HOW TO
DESIGN
A MODEL
RAILROAD

By Lance Mindheim

Kalmbach
Media

Acknowledgments

As they say, there are no new ideas under the sun. I'd like to thank my friends and mentors for providing the framework for everything in this book: Paul Dolkos, Tony Koester, David Barrow, Fred Scheer, Chuck Hitchcock, John King, Keith Jordan, Steve King, Tolga Erbora, and Bill Darnaby. Hopefully I've been able to nudge the bar upwards a little.
—*Lance Mindheim*

On the cover:

A CSX GP38-2 rolls a cut of cars past a container yard on Lance Mindheim's HO Miami East Rail layout. Effective layout planning results in realistic scenes like this one. **Back cover:** Another scene on the Miami layout shows how open areas help call attention to structures and other features. *Two photos: Paul Dolkos*

Kalmbach Media
21027 Crossroads Circle
Waukesha, Wisconsin 53186
www.KalmbachHobbyStore.com

Published in 2021
25 24 23 22 21   1 2 3 4 5

Manufactured in China

ISBN: 978-1-62700-831-0
EISBN: 978-1-62700-832-7

Editor: Jeff Wilson
Book Design: Lisa Schroeder

Library of Congress Control Number: 2020940430

Contents

Young age, hard lesson

As with many of you, the model railroad bug bit me hard when I was in high school. There wasn't an aspect of the hobby or prototype railroading that didn't fascinate me. It was the golden age of publications, and I'd spend hours poring through *Model Railroader*, *Railroad Model Craftsman*, and other hobby magazines.

Hard lessons are often the ones we remember most, and I was fortunate to get my first one early. During my junior year of high school my dad approached me and said, "We really aren't using much of the basement. You can have half of it for your model railroad. I also have some extra lumber you can use for the benchwork." We're talking about half of 800 square feet. (Spoiler alert, there's a phrase for this situation, it's called "having enough rope to hang yourself.")

I jumped in full force. I had limited skills and absolutely no defined scope for the project, but I wanted it all! What could go wrong? By the end of the first weekend I had a relatively massive spaghetti bowl of a track plan whipped up. I wanted this to be a top-flight effort, so of course I wanted mostly handlaid track. The fact that I hadn't ever touched a spike didn't deter me—off I went.

The benchwork went up quickly, crude but functional. Next was the track. Several weekends were spent attempting to handlay about a foot of track. One foot down and only 150 more to go! Weeks went by without getting remotely close to being able to run a train. Slowly the magnitude of

what I had bitten off came home to roost. Progress ground to a halt and eventually the entire venture collapsed. The only factor that provided even the slightest tap on the brakes was that I had very little money to dig an even bigger hole for myself.

I've now been a model railroader for more than 40 years. The poorly planned venture of my high school years was certainly not my last case of less-than-perfect planning. Over the years I'm sure I've made every design mistake discussed in this book and then some. My hope is to pass on some of those hard-learned lessons so you don't have to repeat them.

By profession I'm both a full-time layout designer and a custom layout builder. It's an occupation that gives me a unique perspective of working with a lot of people with varying hobby experience, giving me a real-world understanding of where model railroaders struggle and get hung up during the design process. As a builder, I'm acutely aware that, "what I draw I, and I alone, must build." That position emphasizes the importance that a design be grounded in reality, not fantasy, and ultimately be "buildable."

Applying lessons
I now see the same oncoming headlight when working with other modelers and clients, especially those just entering the hobby. They have, as I had, a lot of pent-up enthusiasm. Many have just retired and have been waiting a lifetime to start their layouts—often having built dozens of structures and other models over the years

while waiting for their dream layout. Adding fuel to the fire, many also have money and a *lot* of space. That sounds fantastic, but left unchecked, it can be a recipe for disaster.

The missing elements? Self-awareness as it relates to their true interests and what they want to get from the hobby, along with a lack of a defined strategy and not having a well-defined project scope. There is often no reality check—there's a lack of recognition that beginners have beginner-level skills and a lack of understanding of how long different construction tasks take. They don't yet have an awareness of where the design and construction landmines and pitfalls are. In short, the beginner is handicapped by not having made enough mistakes. This can all lead to a really rough entry into the hobby. As I write this book, a big part of me is still that 16-year-old trying to pass on those hard-learned lessons of my youth.

Planning vs. design
A primary goal of this book is to differentiate between planning and design—they aren't the same. Planning is an overarching strategy. It's more important and needs to come first. The design is the resulting roadmap for executing the strategy. Not understanding the difference greatly reduces your chances of success.

I'm very sympathetic to the desire to jump right into the X's and O's of drawing sketches and track plans. Taking that shortcut, however, puts you at a very high risk of "correctly drawing the wrong layout." That is, getting a

Knowing exactly what you want from a layout is the key to successfully planning and developing a model railroad design. Following the planning steps was a key in developing realistic scenes like this on my modern-era Miami industrial layout.
Paul Dolkos

design that may be technically correct but deeply flawed in that it doesn't align with your skill level, lifestyle, and true modeling interests. An analogy is a civil engineer trying to decide whether to design an asphalt or concrete road before determining whether the road should even be built in the first place.

We'll be going on a clearly defined step-by-step journey through the planning and design process. By successfully following the steps, the end result will be a well-designed layout. "Well designed" has little to do with the technical minutiae of curve radii and turnout sizes, but instead producing a blueprint for a layout that provides the features, aesthetics, and operational goals you desired.

As we take our journey through the following pages I want to assure you that there is a method to my madness. If you're patient with respect to my emphasis on the importance of strategic planning and gaining an understanding of the tools we have to work with, we will eventually get to what you thought we'd jump into from the beginning: how to put a pen to paper and actually design the track plan.

Why the preamble? In my many decades in the hobby, including the last 20 years as a professional layout designer, I've seen my share of layouts that fell short of expectations and were a disappointment to the owners, including some so frustrating that the individuals left the hobby. In all of these cases, common themes and causes emerged over and over again. First and foremost was a lack of understanding of what the owners wanted the layouts to do for them.

A second landmine is a combination of not understanding how long and complicated layout construction tasks are, the amount of maintenance involved with a layout, and an over-estimation of available free time. Combine this with decades of pent-up enthusiasm and an overriding fear that a layout won't be big enough, and the end result is often biting off way too much model railroad. Enthusiasm can carry you early, but eventually realities hit hard, bringing construction to a screeching halt.

A word on the nuts and bolts of getting a plan to paper: Whether you use a sketch pad, graph paper, pencil, plastic design templates, compass, french curve, ruler, computer track-

planning software, or a combination thereof, is immaterial. Too many modelers get hung up on (to the point of being obsessed with) the mechanics of *drawing* a design instead of the *design* itself. Use the tools you are comfortable with to record an accurate representation.

I've tried to focus on common layout situations and sizes rather than the relatively rare auditorium-filling railroads. Many of the designs in this book are for actual clients and have been built. The principles herein apply to all modeling scales, but most of my examples are in HO—which encompasses the vast majority of plans I work with.

Finally, when dealing with the prototype it goes without saying that, yes, there are exceptions to every rule. The focus of this book will be on the norm, not the exceptions. Now let's turn the page and begin by defining what constitutes a "good" layout design.

1

CHAPTER ONE

Defining a "good" layout design

Planning a model railroad is far more than developing a track plan

My CSX Miami, Fla., East Rail HO layout benefited from having much more clearly defined goals than my previous modeling ventures. I learned from my past mistakes in all facets of the design, with thorough planning from track plan to scenery and structure details.

Before we start to design a model railroad, we need to know the end game—what we're aiming for, **1**. That target, with apologies for such a generic term, is a "good" layout or model railroad design. But what is "good"? Our success, ultimately, is in how we define it.

Let's start out with what good design is *not*. It's not what we typically think of. It's not about whether we use a 24" or 26" minimum radius, no. 6 or no. 8 turnouts, or other technical minutiae. A design isn't just a "track plan." There's a lot more to a model of a railroad than that. Remember that track is just one element, and it needs to dovetail seamlessly with scenery, industries, and structures, both singly and in combination.

Good design *is* about developing an overall layout plan, the drawing of

which is merely a general guide for achieving that.

Ultimately, a good design is one that results in a layout that delivers the degree of enjoyment the owner hoped for going in, **2**, **3**. At the most basic level it really is that simple. However, with some education it's also possible to come up with something that provides even *more* enjoyment than we expected. In addition, thought should be given to our evolving interests and improved skills as we gain experience and immerse ourselves in this great hobby.

Factors of good design

It doesn't matter how technically correct or pretty a drawing looks on paper: If it never gets built or doesn't deliver in some other way, it falls short. What other hobbyists think of it, the degree of exposure it receives, and the number of compliments it gets are all irrelevant. How artistically pleasing to the eye the track plan graphics are is irrelevant. To dig to a deeper level, a good design focuses like a laser on your true interests and passions.

This sounds very basic, and therein lies a trap. Self-awareness of modeling interests isn't always as straightforward as you'd think. To complicate things, interests may change over time. It is absolutely vital that you be crystal clear as to what aspect of the layout will spin out the recreational value you desire. If your passion is scenery building and not operations, then a layout with 150 turnouts probably isn't directed toward your core interests as much as one with a simpler plan and more open, uncluttered vistas for that scenery.

A good design can be brought to a fair level of completion reasonably quickly. It's crucial that the design be buildable. What you draw you must ultimately build—it's not wall art. Keep this in mind as you sketch a four-track grade crossing running through multiple turnouts! The purpose of a design is to serve as a general guide for actually building a layout. And no, most layouts are never

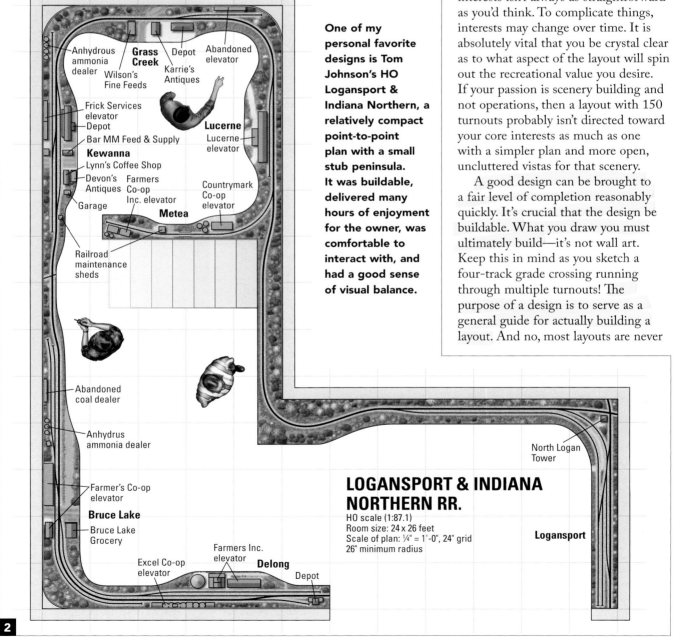

One of my personal favorite designs is Tom Johnson's HO Logansport & Indiana Northern, a relatively compact point-to-point plan with a small stub peninsula. It was buildable, delivered many hours of enjoyment for the owner, was comfortable to interact with, and had a good sense of visual balance.

Anhydrous ammonia dealer

Grass Creek

Wilson's Fine Feeds

Depot

Karrie's Antiques

Abandoned elevator

Frick Services elevator

Depot

Bar MM Feed & Supply

Kewanna

Lynn's Coffee Shop

Devon's Antiques

Farmers Co-op Inc. elevator

Garage

Metea

Lucerne

Lucerne elevator

Countrymark Co-op elevator

Railroad maintenance sheds

Abandoned coal dealer

Anhydrus ammonia dealer

Farmer's Co-op elevator

Bruce Lake

Bruce Lake Grocery

Excel Co-op elevator

Farmers Inc. elevator

Delong

Depot

North Logan Tower

LOGANSPORT & INDIANA NORTHERN RR.

HO scale (1:87.1)
Room size: 24 x 26 feet
Scale of plan: ¼" = 1'-0", 24" grid
26" minimum radius

Logansport

truly "done"—I'm not suggesting otherwise.

What I *am* saying is that the plan should lend itself to having a few trains running between key points and perhaps a completed scene or two within a couple years. If the design is so complex that several years down the road progress has stalled, frustration will set in and you'll lose interest. I've seen it time and time again.

It's important that the complexity of the design match your experience and skill level. It must also take into account not only your available time to work on the layout but also your energy level. You may have several free hours every evening, but if you're exhausted after a long day at work those hours really can't be applied.

A good design minimizes the amount of run length on curves and maximizes run length on straight track. By and large, railroads are linear. Linear designs lend themselves much better to efficient arrangement and composition of towns, yards, and industrial parks. The more "straights" and fewer "curves" the better.

A good design minimizes the number of turnouts, using the least amount to get the job done. Turnout count is one of the driving factors of construction time, construction complexity, layout cost, and maintenance time and expense.

A good design is comfortable to interact with. This can be a subtle trap. In an effort to maximize layout surface area and operational elements, creature comforts are often sacrificed. You may not notice such sacrifices initially when enthusiasm is at its highest. However, over time ergonomic errors and compromises can sap your interest in wanting to deal with the layout. Comfort factors include aisle width,

reach-in distances, duckunders, access to (and amount of) hidden track, adequate lighting, and comfortable layout height. The ability to walk around and follow your train without being cut off by scenery or peninsulas also falls in this category.

Good designs are mechanically reliable. No matter how great a design graphic looks on paper, a layout with compromised mechanical specs that result in derailments or other problems will not be fun to operate. If track elements need to be sacrificed to have appropriate curve radii, turnout sizes, transitions, and grades to increase reliability, so be it.

A good design takes into account the aesthetics of scene composition. A layout can satisfy operational goals and still not be pleasing to look at if it's essentially a three-dimensional schematic. A layout may provide the surface area to satisfy your structure building and scenery passions but if it all doesn't come together using the foundations of effective scene composition, it won't hit the target you're shooting for. Specifically, creating the sense of "being there," of being transported to the time and place that you have in your mind's eye.

Remember that we live in the real world: We have jobs, other hobbies, kids, commutes, and lawns that need to be cut. We have ever-increasing waistlines, decreasing mobility, and too-short arms. Our rooms are never big enough and entry doors and closets always seem to be in the wrong location. Many of us are new to the hobby and at the bottom of the learning curve. This is reality, and these factors are design constraints. Ultimately these constraints and boundaries—and the focus they provide—will prove to be a blessing, not the curse we typically associate with them.

Strategic planning: Know your end game

As modelers, we all share a common bond. It's not just a passion for railroads; it's larger than that. It's a fascination with the rail environment as a whole, the sense of history, the

3

overarching culture that railroads represent, the decades of fond memories spent railside by ourselves or with lifelong friends. It's the fascination we feel when we look at that abandoned depot in the weeds, a fascination that those outside of our circle can't really fully grasp.

In many ways, this is what drives our modeling. It's a desire to be transported, to re-create those mental

Tom Johnson's HO Logansport & Indiana Northern packs a lot of action and detailed scenery on its narrow shelves. This scene, at the elevator at Bruce Lake, is just 18" deep. *Jim Six*

images, the moods they evoke, and bring them into our homes where we can view and relive them at any time, **4**. In one form or another that's usually the end game. The starting point is a strategic plan that gets us there and then uses a design as a vehicle to execute it. The track plan, the design, is simply the means to an end—it's a slippery slope when we assign a greater sense of importance beyond that.

When I think back over the years as to why modelers (including myself) gradually lose interest in a project, it generally doesn't have to do with any glaring technical missteps (although that can be the case too). In most cases, it's because advanced planning—strategic planning—was either given short thrift or completely glossed over. If strategic planning is the vital first step, why is it so often skipped?

Know thyself

The point of making strategic planning your top priority is so that your design is targeted toward and aligns with your core interests and available resources. In other words: Know yourself first and then design toward your true interests and situation.

4

With my HO scale East Rail layout I wanted the sense of being transported to the tropics of Miami. I wanted a layout that would be fairly well detailed but could also be completed in a reasonable timeframe. Finally, I wanted a platform for spinning off 30-minute solo operating sessions.

Exercises in self-awareness aren't as easy as we'd like to think and, for many, probably not as fun. Analyzing our true situations may not yield the realities and answers we want, creating a denial of sorts. Finally, there's often simply a lack of awareness as to how important and vital the subject is or what questions we should be asking ourselves.

As a professional layout designer, I've found that when clients first approach me, the starting point is generally along the lines of "I always liked ABC railroad. I have XYZ space, and 25 kits I've accumulated over the years." The process immediately jumps to a series of hand-drawn sketches, the purpose of which is to take 10 pounds of nails (the desired features) and sledge-hammer them into a 5-pound box (the available space).

The analogy would be a structural engineer who focuses on whether to design a truss or girder bridge to cross a particular stream before considering whether the railroad should even cross that particular stream in the first place.

Strategic planning involves gaining a deep and accurate understanding of what you want the layout to do for you. It's an exercise in self-awareness, something that on the surface seems much easier than it is. Successful planning means understanding clearly what your true modeling interests are so you can focus like a laser and design toward them. It also takes into account an accurate assessment of your true resources.

5

Many of my layouts were traditional in the sense that they modeled a region or a large section of a specific place, and were set up to support "formal" operating sessions. Layouts don't have to be "traditional" though. My HO Los Angeles Junction layout was a departure from the norm in that I simply wanted a piece of 3D wall art I could look at. It only has two turnouts. *Paul Dolkos*

The answer lies in the questions

The following exercise can be helpful. Ask yourself the following questions, and be detailed and honest in your answers. I've added follow-up questions to most to help guide you. Note that in most cases these questions deal with a spectrum rather than absolutes.

- **Where is your enjoyment going to come from? Do you want the sense of being transported to a meaningful time and place?** Saying "I want to model Omaha, Neb., in 1955" isn't strategic planning. Saying "I grew up in Omaha in the mid- 1950s and have many meaningful memories going trackside with my father and friends. The crews used to let me ride in the cab. I want the sense of going back to that time and place" provides a firm foundation for a plan.

- **Is your primary interest the "satisfaction" of assembly?** If so, assembling what? Structures? Rolling stock? Scenery? Composing and arranging entire scenes? If this is where your enjoyment comes from, and it is for many, do you need a track plan with more than 100 turnouts to spurs you really have no interest in operating?

- **Do you want to look at the layout as you would a painting?** This is important because for many—the builders among us—when they are honest with themselves are far more ambivalent about trains in motion than they realize (or admit). The actual answer is far less important than the accurate answer.

- **Do you want to simply *watch* trains in motion, or *interact* with them?** In other words, are you a railfan or operator? If you're primarily a railfan, what types of scenes and back stories do you want to watch unfold? If you're an operator, what type do you

enjoy: Over the road (main line)? Branch line? Industrial switching? Yard switching? A combination?

- **How important are prototypical operations to you?** How far do you want to take operational accuracy? Accurate to the point of simulating air tests and having a timetable and written train orders, or just to do some switching and catch the flavor of prototype operations?

- **How often will you operate the layout?** Do you plan to run it by yourself, or with others (how many)? How long will your sessions last? Thirty minutes of solo time? Three hours with a crew (the max for most people if they're honest)? How do you want to switch cars: prototypically slowly, including setting brakes? A middle ground?

- **How passionate and deeply immersed are you in the hobby?** Are you a casual recreationalist, or a die-hard where the hobby is a major source of life satisfaction? Will your required financial commitment reflect this?

- **How much time do you have to work on the layout?** More accurately, how much energy do you have? Having two hours of free time in the evening doesn't do you much good if you're totally exhausted after work.

- **What's your skill level?** How many layouts have you built? Said less diplomatically: Have you made enough mistakes and gained enough experience to truly grasp how long specific tasks take and how long different scenes and track arrangements take to build?
- **How interested are you in improving your skill level?** Be honest.
- **How long will you be in your present house or dwelling?**
- **Do you want to "build" a layout or "have" a layout?** Meaning: Do you enjoy the process of creating or do you just want to have a finished product as soon as possible?
- **How high is your interest in photography?** If it's high you'll want to take that into account when designing your scenes.
- **How much layout do you want completed at different milestones?** At one year? Two years? For example, is it important that at least some trains be running 12 months after starting the layout?
- **What aspects of the hobby do you enjoy the *least*?** You probably want to design in fewer of those.
- **What is your modeling speed?** This tends to remain constant once basic skills are achieved.
- **Are highly detailed scenes vital to you or is the "good enough" standard fine?**
- **Do you want to model one place or a combination of places?** Do you want to model just what happens at Town A, or do you want to model the journey from Town A to Town B and even to Towns C and D?
- **How much layout do you want to bite off in terms of complexity and just plain old construction time?** This is a vital question. Without a history of previous layouts under your belt, this can be a difficult question to answer. I've seen many modelers get into trouble with this early.

Defining your vision

Your layout design should be largely skewed toward your specific interests. If you are a "let em' cruise" railfan, you probably don't need a design with lots of turnouts and complex trackwork, **5.** If prototypical operation is your passion, scenery and scene composition may not be as vital, **6.** Start by defining your vision, specifying what you *really* want the layout to do for you.

It's common for a design to start with something along the lines of "I want a layout with a coal mine, pier, and turntable." Or, for a prototype modeler, "I want to model the XYZ prototype between towns A and B." That's where the trouble starts, because statements like those don't really address and strike at the core of what you're trying to do. This results in layouts that aren't as fulfilling as they could be, are visually unbalanced, difficult to build, or just simply put you in a position of realizing after it's done that you've somehow missed the target in a hard-to-define way.

An example of a clear objective would be: "I want to capture the cadence of the operations of XYZ railroad between towns A and C. I want to operate monthly, have sessions that last three hours, and support three or four crews. I'm ambivalent about scenery and structures. I'd like the layout up and hosting operating sessions in 18 months."

Another would be: "I want to be transported to the 'feel and character' of XYZ railroad between A and C. While I kind of enjoy operations, I can take them or leave them. I love structure building and scenery, and want to sit back, take in, and be transported to what I remember of that prototype. I want one scene done in 18 months and don't really care how long it takes to complete the rest."

In working with a variety of modelers, I've found what most of us want ultimately is that sense of being transported to a different time and place when we look at our layouts and/ or operate them. The more clearly we can articulate the specifics of that end game, the more effective and successful the resulting layout will be.

The challenge is that often what we truly want is buried so deeply in our subconscious that we have a hard time spelling it out for ourselves. It's not easy. It becomes harder when we realize that saying you want to model the X&Z railroad between A and B in 1955 is a shortcut that isn't specific enough. It's much easier and fun to just say, "the heck with it, I just want to draw some track diagrams." Too easily, that can become the natural default, and doing so puts us in a position of running full speed in the wrong direction down a one-way street.

Here's an actual example. One of my clients wanted to model Thurmond, W.Va., in the present day, **7.** He was rare in that he could clearly explain what his vision for the layout was. Here's his summary:

"There is a definite mood/feeling I am looking for. I grew up in Minnesota with long winters, and I suppose like most kids summer was my favorite. I spent a lot of time as a kid on the Mississippi river. I distinctly remember the lush green of the trees contrasted with the light-colored sand at the river's edge, the dirty water, and the colors of the brick and concrete of the Anoka bridge as I went under it hundreds of times.

"To me, Appalachian scenery is similar in terms of the colors and contrasts. The lush green canopy, the light-colored track ballast, sand on the river banks, the faded brick and the old concrete colors of the buildings, and of course the colors of the trains rolling through those scenes.

"I've subscribed to Model Railroader *off and on over the years, and I've intently studied every Appalachian-themed railroad article. Allen McClelland's original Virginian & Ohio has always been the benchmark of Appalachian model railroads for me. I know he sort of takes a "close enough" approach to modelling and is mostly focused on operations, but he's one heck of an artist in my opinion. The photos of his railroad that capture me the most are the ones that appear to be from a sunny day. In fact, when I look at those drone videos, the scenes that capture me the most are the sunny-day scenes. The exact same buildings in the same video just a few seconds apart with overcast skies are less appealing.*

"So I guess the mood/feeling I'm trying to capture is from those warm, sunny,

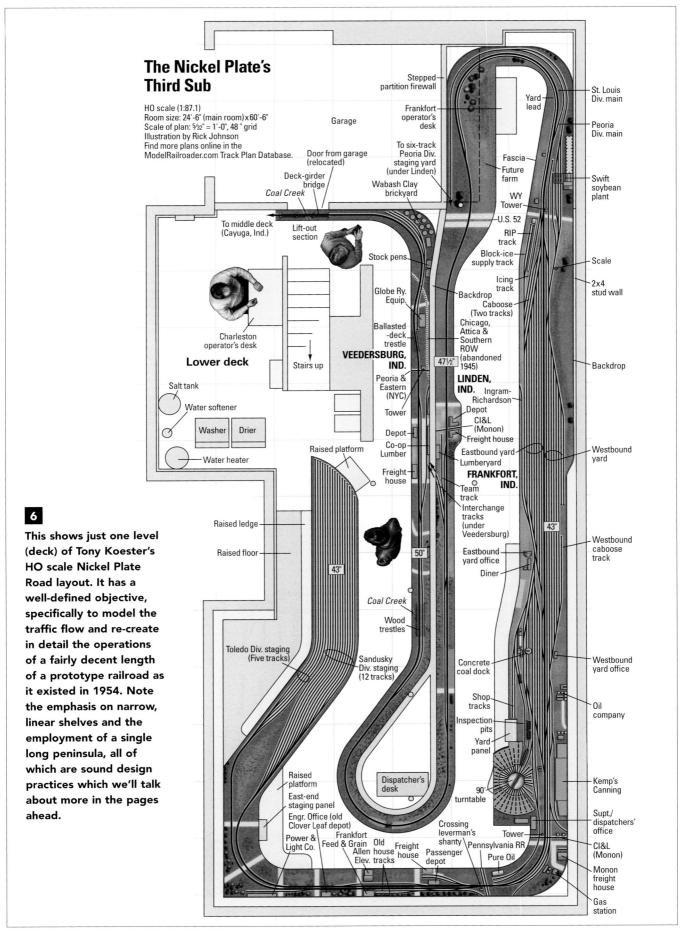

The Nickel Plate's Third Sub

HO scale (1:87.1)
Room size: 24'-6" (main room) x 60'-6"
Scale of plan: 5/32" = 1'-0", 48" grid
Illustration by Rick Johnson
Find more plans online in the
ModelRailroader.com Track Plan Database.

Garage

Stepped partition firewall

Frankfort operator's desk

To six-track Peoria Div. staging yard (under Linden)

Wabash Clay brickyard

Door from garage (relocated)

Deck-girder bridge

Coal Creek

Lift-out section

To middle deck (Cayuga, Ind.)

Stock pens

Globe Ry. Equip.

Ballasted-deck trestle

VEEDERSBURG, IND.

Peoria & Eastern (NYC)

Tower

Depot

Co-op Lumber

Freight house

Charleston operator's desk

Lower deck

Stairs up

Salt tank

Water softener

Washer   Drier

Water heater

Raised platform

Raised ledge

Raised floor

43"

50"

Coal Creek

Wood trestles

Toledo Div. staging (Five tracks)

Sandusky Div. staging (12 tracks)

Raised platform
East-end staging panel
Engr. Office (old Clover Leaf depot)

Power & Light Co.

Frankfort Feed & Grain

Allen Elev.

Old house tracks

Freight house

Dispatcher's desk

Crossing leverman's shanty

Passenger depot

Pennsylvania RR
Pure Oil

St. Louis Div. main

Peoria Div. main

Yard lead

Fascia
Future farm

WY Tower

U.S. 52

RIP track

Block-ice supply track

Icing track

Backdrop

Caboose (Two tracks)

Chicago, Attica & Southern ROW (abandoned 1945)

47½"

LINDEN, IND.

Ingram-Richardson Depot

CI&L (Monon)

Freight house

Eastbound yard

Lumberyard

FRANKFORT, IND.

Team track

Interchange tracks (under Veedersburg)

Eastbound yard office

Diner

Swift soybean plant

Scale

2x4 stud wall

Backdrop

Westbound yard

Westbound caboose track

Westbound yard office

Oil company

Kemp's Canning

Supt./ dispatchers' office

CI&L (Monon)

Monon freight house

Gas station

Concrete coal dock

Shop tracks

Inspection pits

Yard panel

90' turntable

43"

Tower

6

This shows just one level (deck) of Tony Koester's HO scale Nickel Plate Road layout. It has a well-defined objective, specifically to model the traffic flow and re-create in detail the operations of a fairly decent length of a prototype railroad as it existed in 1954. Note the emphasis on narrow, linear shelves and the employment of a single long peninsula, all of which are sound design practices which we'll talk about more in the pages ahead.

carefree days I spent as a kid on the Mississippi river. The colors and contrasts are extremely important to me to create such a warm looking scene that is easy on the eyes.

"The colors of the locomotives are important to me. For the last 10 years, I've really been drawn into CSX's color schemes. Maybe it's because the V&O color scheme was blue. The BNSF color schemes I see in my area of Minnesota have never appealed to me at all. But, I do get to see CSX locos here from time to time, and those always grab my attention."

He was very clear on what his interests were and were not. Essentially he wanted a three-dimensional piece of animated art, a rendition of the iconic Thurmond scene with trains running through it. He had no interest in operations of any sort or in modeling any other places. This clear focus set him up for success as shown in the finished layout plan, **8**, and modeled scene, **9**.

Designing toward your target: your interests

The top of the planning hierarchy is, as we just discussed, truly understanding what you want the layout to do for you. One step down from that is understanding what aspects of the hobby you enjoy the most. What type of modeler are you?

The purpose of this thought exercise is to come away with a sense of where your core interests lie so you can design toward that target. I've seen many modelers skip this step. I often see designs that include features and areas of focus that aren't really aligned with a modeler's main interests. The consequence is wasted time and expense on areas they don't care about, as well as less space for elements that *are* of interest.

Most of us are on a spectrum and hold a variety of interests to some degree so it's generally not an all-or-nothing affair. Over the years I've

found that major layout interests lie in the following areas:
- Railfanning (watching trains roll by)
- Structure building
- Scenery building
- Rolling stock/locomotives (the layout as a display platform for locomotives and cars)
- Scene composition (combining multiple elements into specific scenes)
- Art viewing/movie watching (wants to be "transported" to a time and place that is personally meaningful—this may or may not be strictly prototypical, and owner may not care if trains are moving)
- Operations

Let's look at some of these groups in detail.

Railfans: Many modelers just want to be railfans. Their enjoyment comes from simply watching trains in motion, with different locomotive lashups and varying train consists running against a

7

This is the iconic scene in Thurmond, W.Va., that my client wanted to capture. A Chesapeake & Ohio locomotive and caboose roll through the town in 1983. *Paul Dolkos*

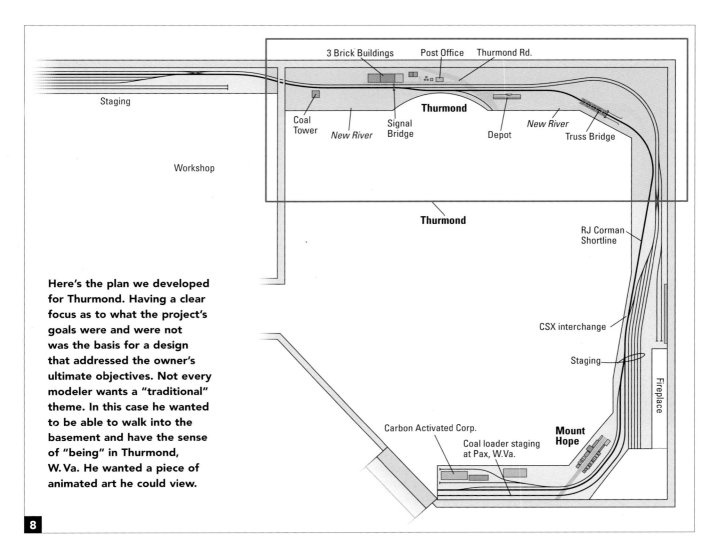

3 Brick Buildings   Post Office   Thurmond Rd.

Staging

Coal Tower   New River   Signal Bridge   **Thurmond**   Depot   New River   Truss Bridge

Workshop

Thurmond

RJ Corman Shortline

CSX interchange

Staging

Fireplace

Here's the plan we developed for Thurmond. Having a clear focus as to what the project's goals were and were not was the basis for a design that addressed the owner's ultimate objectives. Not every modeler wants a "traditional" theme. In this case he wanted to be able to walk into the basement and have the sense of "being" in Thurmond, W. Va. He wanted a piece of animated art he could view.

Carbon Activated Corp.

Coal loader staging at Pax, W.Va.

Mount Hope

8

backdrop of pleasing scenery. This can include modelers who enjoy detailing and weathering locomotives and rolling stock and just watching them run. For these modelers, a conscious effort should be made to simplify trackwork and allow ample square footage for scenic vistas, **10**.

Scenery and structures: For a large percentage of hobbyists, a primary source of enjoyment is structure and/ or scenery construction. If this is you, be wary of including track that serves no purpose in terms of your main interests. Remember that layout design is not just "track planning"—it's scene planning. If scenery and structures are your thing, make sure you have adequate and well-planned areas for them.

The Time Machine: For many, a specific location and time is especially meaningful, and being transported

back in time to this location is an overriding goal. Here, scene composition takes on a more crucial role because these modelers want to feel like they are there. Even if their interest in operations is minimal, track takes on the role of a visual prop whether they want to actually switch it or not. If it was there in real life, it should be on the plan. The subtle distinction here is that the role of track is visual first, operational second. Of course, some of these same modelers also want the operational aspect as well.

Operators

Let's look at operators in depth. Operating a layout prototypically is one of the more interesting aspects of the hobby for many. This could play out in miniature via mainline timetable-and-train-order scenarios, single-train branchline operations, industrial switching, or a mix of all of these. For operators, the visual aspect and scene composition may take a back seat to track arrangements that enhance operations. Many are totally content with the proverbial "Plywood Pacific" because their enjoyment

More than a track plan

Layout design encompasses far more than track arrangements and positioning. It also relates to the elements the track runs through, scenery planning, the defining characteristics of the industries the track serves in terms of size, collections of structures, placement of structures, and overall industry selection in general.

This is the completed model of the Thurmond scene I built for the customer (photographed under real sky).

comes from the chess-game aspect of realistically moving trains.

For these modelers, a key aspect of design is thinking through what you want an operating session to look like so that you have the necessary track infrastructure in place to support it. Classification yard and staging yard design, siding location and size, number of towns, and number of industrial spurs are all things that need to be carefully considered and planned. When envisioning an operating session, ask yourself how long you want it to run, how many crews you want to have (and how many people in a crew), and what specifically each will be doing.

A major planning consideration—and one that few think enough about—is the desired length of an operating session. When operators plan their layouts, typically a prototype railroad, region, and then several specific places are chosen, and an effort made to copy the existing track as closely as possible. That is all well and good.

However, such an approach misses a key ingredient: the human attention

span. Specifically, how long do you and your operators want a session to last before burnout begins to set in? Failing to consider this runs the risk of building far more capacity into a layout than you can ever hope to utilize in a session. The end result is a layout that is larger than it needs to be, takes too long to build, has more track than necessary, has more compromises than it needs to have, and is unnecessarily expensive and maintenance intensive.

Anecdotally I've noticed that many modelers grossly underestimate how often they'll be running trains by themselves as opposed to having a full operating crew. In my experience, a solo session can run about 30 to 60 minutes before I've had enough. While there are "op-til-you-drop" die-hards, by and large my experience with crews is that after two and a half to three hours most people start to lose interest.

Do you really need a layout that can spin off five hours of solo operating, given that you'll never utilize it? Do you need a crew-based layout that could would take seven, eight, or nine real-time hours to fully utilize the capacity? While you do want enough

capacity to provide variety from session to session, keep in mind that the prototype by and large does the same things operationally week in and week out.

My usual recommendation is to consider building in enough capacity for your most commonly desired session length plus a small cushion for some variety. Then it may be time to hit the brakes and stop adding more track to the design. Another way of looking at it: figure out how long you want a session to last, build in a cushion, and design your track density toward that time figure.

There's a tendency to overestimate how often we'll be having "formal" sessions, or how often we'll even operate, period. It's wise to make provisions in the design to support interesting solo operating scenarios so you can grab a throttle on your own.

If you're planning for sessions that require multiple operators or crews, try to visualize a session and determine how many operators you'll need. Layouts that take 15 people or more to operate do exist and run successfully. However, that's a lot to

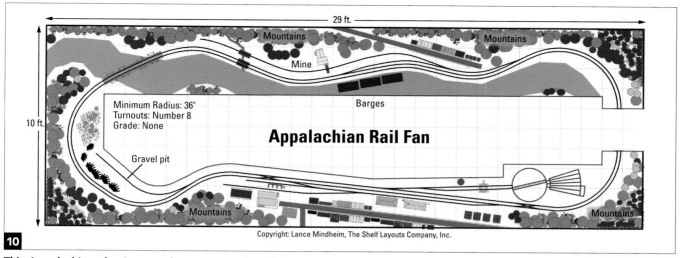

10

Within the image: 29 ft., Mountains, Mountains, Mine, Barges, 10 ft., Minimum Radius: 36" / Turnouts: Number 8 / Grade: None, **Appalachian Rail Fan**, Gravel pit, Mountains, Mountains

This Appalachian plan is geared more toward modelers with an interest in railfanning and scenery and structure building as opposed to operations. It has a double-track main line, no staging, and relatively simple construction.

people to round up month in and month out. If you build a layout that size, will you be able recruit a crew to man it? Consistently? Consistently after the novelty of the layout has worn off? Maybe yes, maybe no, but it's a question worth asking. I've known people who built large operations-based layouts, only to be frustrated trying to get enough operators.

Finally, as your knowledge of prototype operations increase and you incorporate more and more of those real-world practices, it will take less and less track to keep you happily entertained. Just be careful: A little excess capacity provides variety and is nice. Too much capacity is wasteful and creates problems of its own from extended layout construction time and cost to increased maintenance.

Managing complexity

A crucial part of the planning process is understanding the concept of complexity, and then using that knowledge to your advantage and to keep you out of trouble, **11, 12**. Although related, size and complexity aren't the same thing. Layout size is self-explanatory and relates primarily to the square footage of your benchwork. Complexity refers to the time and difficulty associated with building a specific feature or combination of features. It relates to things such as the number of turnouts, complex track features, and whether

you use flextrack or hand-lay track, **13**. It also involves the number of and detail level of your structures and other scenic features.

A 20-foot-long scene running through grass fields is large but not complex. The same scene comprising deep canyons, complex rock formations, and raging rapids could take 10 times as long to build. Likewise, a small town with a few agricultural structures might come together in a few months; a 20-square-foot city scene could take several years to build.

Early in the process there has to be an appreciation for the direct relationship between how detailed or complex you want an area to be and how much—*realistically*—you can build at that detail level. Once you gain that awareness, you then need to apply that reality to your desired layout size. This is particularly important for modelers who derive their satisfaction from creating detailed models, whether it be handlaid track, scratchbuilt structures, or intricate scenery. In simple terms, taking the number of features you have on a layout and then multiplying that by how long it takes to build them will tell you how long it will take to build a layout or a scene. Ideally we want a balance of interesting projects and consistent construction progress.

Factors of complexity include:
- Turnout count
- Layout square footage and benchwork width

- Grades
- Urban scenery (amount and level of detail)
- Amount of vertical scenery relief and scenery complexity (detailed rock formations, waterways, etc.)
- Bridges, viaducts, and trestles
- Double-track main lines
- Multiple decks
- Complex and/or handlaid trackwork

Age and experience factor in as well. The two most common entry points to the hobby are those in their teens/early 20s and recent retirees. Unlike a cash-starved teen with limited space, the retiree often has ample resources in terms of a large available space and a deep pocketbook. On the surface that may seem like a good thing, but more often than not it ends up being a case of having a bigger shovel to dig a bigger hole for yourself. Just because you have the space and money to build a large, complex model railroad doesn't mean you should, particularly if you've yet to acquire the skills to do so without getting bogged down.

Having room for a large layout would appear to be a blessing. You can have longer mainline runs, more scenes, and more space between scenes. A problem arises, however, when a modeler doesn't have a clear understanding of what such an undertaking entails. Sadly, I've seen person after person become engulfed and overwhelmed because they underestimated the magnitude of their

12

The complex trackwork at St. Louis Union Depot would make an impressive model scene. It would also require a tremendous amount of space and take a lot of time (and skill) to build. Here a Gulf, Mobile & Ohio train backs into its track at the train shed in 1950. *Don Sims*

This Christmas 1968 scene of Washington's Union Station is as compelling as they come. It's also very complex, with lots of intricate trackwork and overhead wire for electric operations. Choosing to model something like this should be entered into with one's eyes wide open.
Paul Dolkos

dreams. Sometimes such ambitious projects never get to the point where trains can run, let alone having any finished scenes.

Maintenance and progress

Modelers often grossly underestimate layout maintenance. Layouts—especially large ones—are complex machines with many moving parts. Components wear out and fail, and dust accumulates on rails, structures, and scenery. Lumber expands, contracts, and shifts, and along with that the track above, creating kinks and other issues that need to be adjusted. Scenery colors fade and water effects become dull. You must ask yourself if you truly understand what will be involved in maintaining your project (assuming you even get it built).

Also, in order to maintain enthusiasm, you need to see progress, to see a portion of your vision come together. How long are you prepared to wait for this? Track is one thing; ballast, scenery, and structures are another. It may take an experienced modeler many months just to scenic a 20-square-foot scene. If it takes four months of your available time to build that highly detailed paper mill, how long will it take to put even a dent in the rest of your structure list? And don't forget roadways and sidewalks, which can take as long to build as the structures themselves. And remember that large layouts take lots freight cars and locomotives, all of which need to have couplers adjusted, weight added, and for locomotives, wiring programmed and tuned.

Even if you do have the necessary construction skills, there are hard limits on how fast we can build. Highly detailed subjects take time to model, and lots of it. You need to apply the reality check of how long things will take to build versus the size of your potential layout. If you want to fill a 20 x 40-foot basement, it is unrealistic to expect to handlay highly detailed track with individual tie plates and

On my Los Angeles Junction layout I *thought* I wanted all handlaid track, including photo-etched tie plates, wood ties, and individual spikes. I took that approach with the track on the right of the photo. The track on the left is Micro Engineering flextrack. There wasn't enough of a visual difference to justify continuing with the handlaid program and the time it entailed. By managing complexity and shifting to flextrack, construction time sped up and my enthusiasm for the layout notched up.

Gerry Leone is a strong proponent of allowing breathing space between elements. His HO Bona Vista layout has busy, detailed city and town scenes separated by open spaces and flowing scenery. *Gerry Leone*

15

My Downtown Spur layout is fairly large and was complex to build owing to its urban theme. To see progress and maintain interest, I first limited the turnout count to only 13. Second, I quickly laid down temporary flextrack to get the layout running. I also started with simple mockups of the structures. I then went back later and, at my leisure, laid more-detailed track and replaced the mockups with the final structure models.

joint bars and get it finished. If you're an urban modeler and it takes you two months to build a structure and another month to detail the surrounding pavement, sidewalks, and utilities, is it realistic to have dozens of additional city structures pending and hope to complete them?

To get a layout built, you'll need to manage the complexity of your features, the size of your benchwork footprint, or both so you can maintain

momentum and see progress, **14, 15**.

Here some ways to manage complexity:
• Limit the number and/or size of complex features
• Reduce the overall size of the layout
• Keep benchwork width narrow (we tend to make it much wider than necessary to attain our visual goals)
• Avoid grades unless they serve an operational purpose (such as helper locomotives)

• Reduce the detail level of some or all of your features (Tony Koester's "good enough" approach applies an 80/20 rule: the first 20 percent of effort and detail levels produce 80 percent of the visual impact)
• Use structure mockups as visual stand-ins; replace them later with more-detailed models at your leisure
• Use flextrack on most of the layout and only use more detailed track in key scenes
• Accept that some key scenes will be finished and some in all likelihood will remain unfinished

Just as we need to be aware of design elements that build upon one another to make a layout too complex,

we can also play the flip side to our advantage. Specifically, those with limited space and small layouts can do the opposite, **16**. They can *increase* complexity to increase build time. Just as "big" doesn't mean "better" or "more fun," "small" doesn't mean "compromise" or "less fun."

The reason? Layout success is measured simply by the hours of

16

My N Scale Brooklyn Terminal layout is small by any measure. I consciously increased construction time by focusing on more-detailed features such as street running (top) and handlaid code 40 track (above).

This plan is well-suited for somebody with ample space but entry-level skills. It's not small by any means but would be fairly simple to build. It's a point-to-point plan with a hidden connector to allow continuous running.

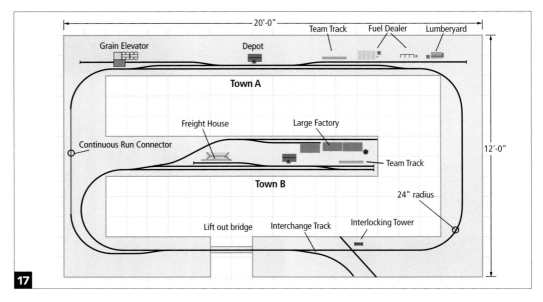

17

A key decision is how much of our theme we choose to model; where we set our boundaries. For any given length of mainline run we have two options: We can have more (but smaller) towns packed closely together, or fewer but larger towns with more space between them.

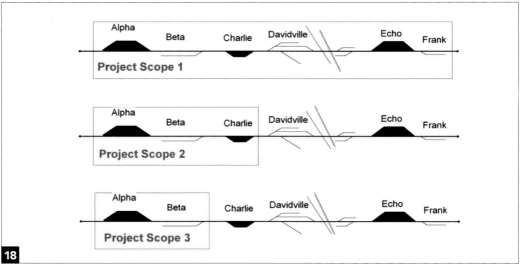

18

My CSX Downtown Spur layout not only focuses on a single town—Miami—it represents just a small portion of that place (right). By limiting the scope, the resulting point-to-point plan (opposite page) is able to capture a number of industries, buildings, and other features without feeling crowded.

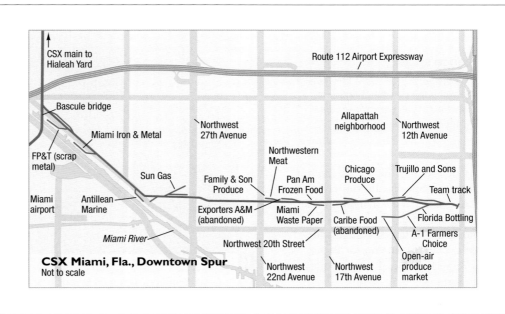

19

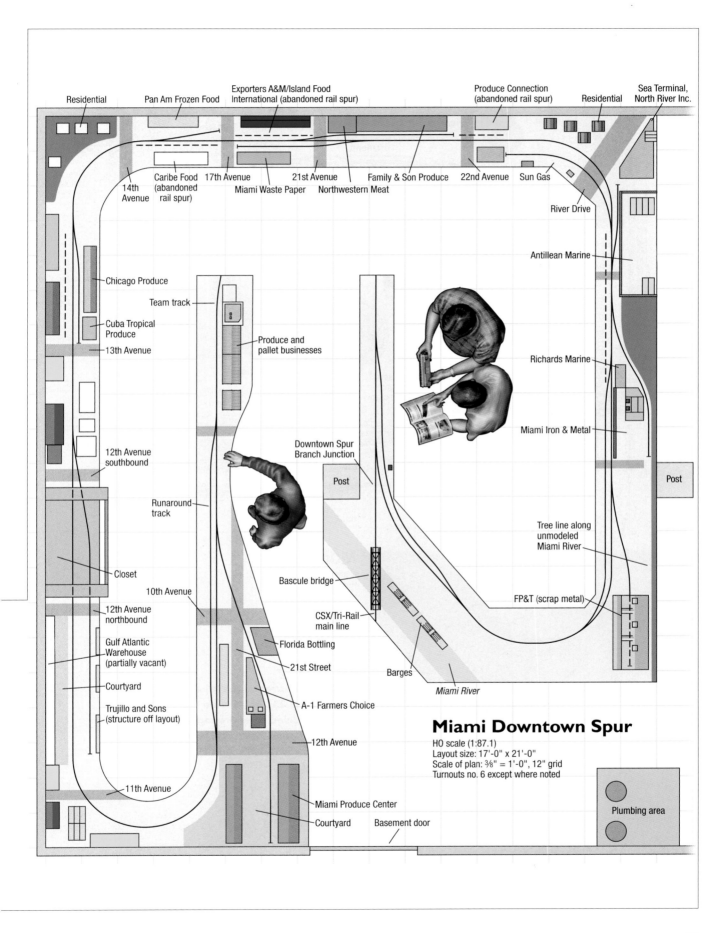

Residential Pan Am Frozen Food Exporters A&M/Island Food International (abandoned rail spur) Produce Connection (abandoned rail spur) Residential Sea Terminal, North River Inc.

14th Avenue Caribe Food (abandoned rail spur) 17th Avenue 21st Avenue Family & Son Produce 22nd Avenue Sun Gas

Miami Waste Paper Northwestern Meat

River Drive

Antillean Marine

Chicago Produce

Team track

Cuba Tropical Produce

Produce and pallet businesses

13th Avenue

Richards Marine

12th Avenue southbound

Miami Iron & Metal

Downtown Spur Branch Junction

Post

Runaround track

Post

Tree line along unmodeled Miami River

Closet

10th Avenue

Bascule bridge

12th Avenue northbound

FP&T (scrap metal)

CSX/Tri-Rail main line

Gulf Atlantic Warehouse (partially vacant)

Florida Bottling

Courtyard

21st Street

Barges

Trujillo and Sons (structure off layout)

A-1 Farmers Choice

Miami River

12th Avenue

Miami Downtown Spur

11th Avenue

HO scale (1:87.1)
Layout size: 17'-0" x 21'-0"
Scale of plan: ⅜" = 1'-0", 12" grid
Turnouts no. 6 except where noted

Miami Produce Center

Courtyard Basement door

Plumbing area

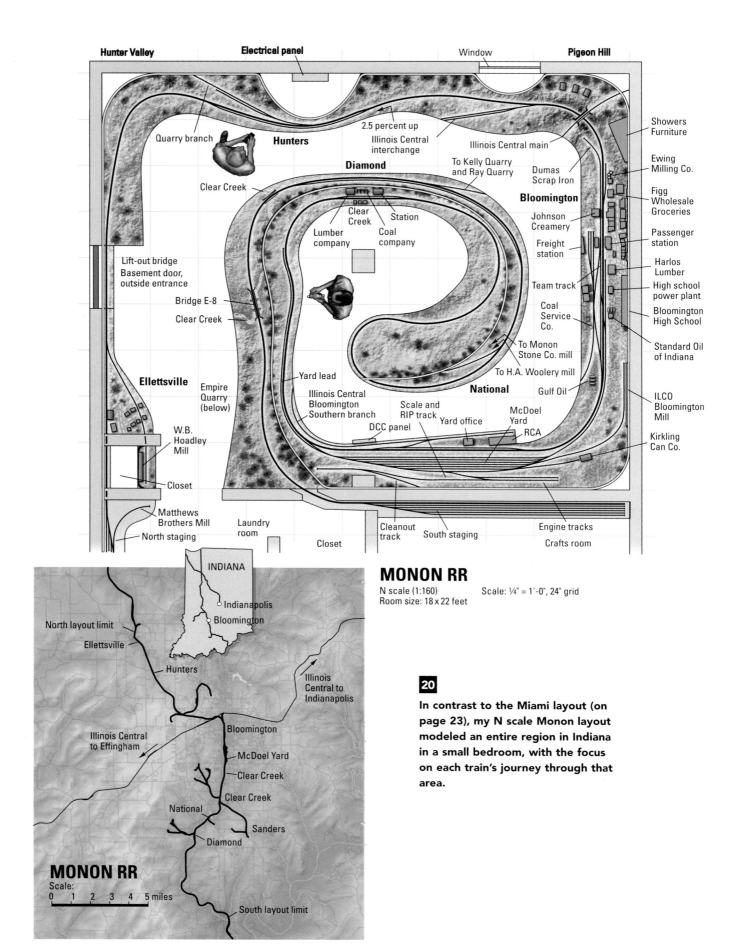

Hunter Valley **Electrical panel** Window **Pigeon Hill**

Showers
Furniture

Quarry branch **Hunters**

2.5 percent up

Illinois Central
interchange

Illinois Central main

To Kelly Quarry
and Ray Quarry

Dumas
Scrap Iron

Ewing
Milling Co.

Figg
Wholesale
Groceries

Diamond

Clear Creek

Bloomington

Johnson
Creamery

Clear
Creek

Station

Passenger
station

Freight
station

Lumber
company

Coal
company

Harlos
Lumber

Team track

High school
power plant

**Lift-out bridge
Basement door,
outside entrance**

Coal
Service
Co.

Bloomington
High School

Bridge E-8

To Monon
Stone Co. mill

Standard Oil
of Indiana

Clear Creek

To H.A. Woolery mill

Gulf Oil

Ellettsville

Empire
Quarry
(below)

Yard lead

National

ILCO
Bloomington
Mill

Illinois Central
Bloomington
Southern branch

Scale and
RIP track

Yard office

McDoel
Yard

Kirkling
Can Co.

W.B.
Hoadley
Mill

DCC panel

RCA

Closet

Matthews
Brothers Mill

North staging

Laundry
room

Closet

Cleanout
track

South staging

Engine tracks

Crafts room

MONON RR

N scale (1:160)   Scale: ¼" = 1'-0", 24" grid
Room size: 18 x 22 feet

INDIANA

Indianapolis

Bloomington

North layout limit

Ellettsville

Hunters

Illinois
Central to
Indianapolis

Illinois Central
to Effingham

Bloomington

McDoel Yard

Clear Creek

Clear Creek

National

Sanders

Diamond

MONON RR

Scale:
0 1 2 3 4 5 miles

South layout limit

20

In contrast to the Miami layout (on
page 23), my N scale Monon layout
modeled an entire region in Indiana
in a small bedroom, with the focus
on each train's journey through that
area.

This pleasant scene on Bob Lucas' HO Akron, Canton & Youngstown sets a mood for the journeys of the trains that pass through it. *Chris Lantz*

enjoyment provided. Smaller footprints allow the luxury of not feeling the time pressure to build vast amounts of square footage, track, and scenic features. You can sit back, relax, and focus on detail work. You can take the time to do superdetailing and still see progress. You can have highly detailed structures and rolling stock because you don't need that many of them.

Large space, small skills

Just because a layout is large doesn't mean it has to be complex. Early success and momentum is crucial, especially for newcomers trying to maintain passion for the hobby. You can have a relatively large layout in terms of square footage and run length and design it in a way that it is easy to build, **17**. If you are a newcomer you want to set yourself up for success, and the key to success is to keep the first effort simple: something that falls together easily.

This plan occupies a relatively large space, but it's designed to be very simple to build and operationally sophisticated. It's an opportunity for a hobbyist to get up and going quickly and learn new skills. If you build this design, you won't be bored, I promise! If you outgrow it after several years, then it would be simple to keep the benchwork in place, and build something new on top of it.

Journey or destination?

You'll see that "know thyself" is an ongoing theme of the planning process. The clearer you truly are as to what you

enjoy and what you want a layout to do for you, the more likely you are to hit your mark. If you don't know what you want, then success becomes an exercise in hoping you get lucky.

A key question to answer early on is whether you want to model the journey or the destination. Do you want to model the transportation process of a train going from town A to B to C, **18**, or, do you just want to model what happens at C, **19**? This matters, and it matters a *lot*.

A "journey" modeler enjoys watching the trip, **20**, **21**. These modelers enjoy the operational theater associated with multiple trains going about their work without having cornfield meets. A "destination" modeler may have fond memories of one specific town and want to be transported to that place and it alone. He may have limited space. He may prefer switching operations over mainline operations.

Making decisions

To wrap this section up and put things in context, let's take a look at the decisions we must make and where they fit into the planning hierarchy. Some we've just discussed; others are coming the pages ahead. Here are strategic questions to ask yourself:
- **What do I want the layout to do for me?** Where will I derive my satisfaction? Do I want to feel transported to a time and place,

essentially viewing it as I would a piece of art? Do I want to just sit back and watch trains in motion through a backdrop of scenes with little interaction (railfan style)? Do I want to interact with trains in motion (operations)? Is my primary source of enjoyment the act of building things, whether it be structures, scenery, or rolling stock?
- **How much layout do I want to bite off in terms of size?**
- **How complex do I want my layout to be?** How much do I want to have done at specific milestones in the future? How do I manage complexity so there is an alignment between my time and skills and the progress I'd like to see it specific points in time?
- **How much time and energy do I realistically have to apply to the hobby?**
- **What is my current skill level?** Am I satisfied with the status quo or do I want to work to add to my skill set?
- **How many towns do I want?** Do I want to model the journey or the destination?
- **How long do I want operating sessions to run?**

A strategically well-planned layout will be one that hones in on and clearly aligns with the answers to these questions.

CHAPTER TWO

How the prototype does "track planning"

Follow full-size railroads to achieve realistic modeled track arrangements

A westbound Florida East Coast double-stack train approaches IRIS crossing in Miami on Thanksgiving Day, 2014. This image exemplifies modern railroad efficiency at its best.
Tolga Erbora

We model—or copy in miniature—actual railroads because we are fascinated by their cadence, rhythm, atmosphere, and operations, **1**. To that extent it makes sense to have at least a cursory knowledge of what they do, how they do it, and why they do things the way they do. It would take volumes of books to even scratch the surface of the railroad business and its operational structure, but let's look at some key factors that particularly apply to model railroad design.

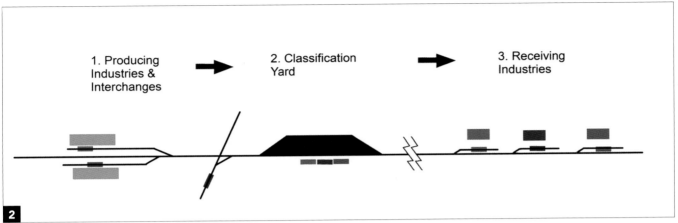

1. Producing Industries & Interchanges → 2. Classification Yard → 3. Receiving Industries

2

At the most basic level, cars loaded with a commodity are collected from "industries," moved to, sorted, and grouped in a yard according to their final destination, moved back out over the main line in a manner that avoids trains coming in the opposing direction, and then delivered to the customer.

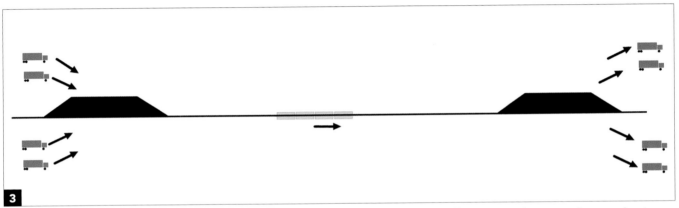

3

In modern times it's becoming increasingly common for single commodities and traffic types such as containers and auto racks to be brought to a specialized yard by truck, loaded on a hotshot, non-stop train, then delivered to a receiving yard hundreds or thousands of miles away.

How accurately you choose to copy what the big boys do is a personal decision each modeler needs to make. This should be driven solely by what you find interesting and enjoyable, and not by any outside pressure of how you should do things. However, even those who are not strict prototype modelers still want layouts that are plausible—something that is believable.

Many of the design challenges we modelers face have been worked out in full scale by design engineers for prototype railroads. With each passing year more information becomes available in terms of aerial photos and maps that have been digitized and posted online. Simply copying what prototype railroads did in a given area or situation can be a real ace in the hole and possible roadmap to a design solution.

Although railroading's business model has changed over time, the essential role of a railroad is simple: move really heavy and/or bulky stuff long distances more cheaply than trucks can, **2.** The heavier the commodity and longer the distance, the more efficient rail becomes. The nature of what railroads do and don't do has evolved over the decades and will continue to do so. We've seen the change from single boxcars loaded at a siding being replaced by containers and large-scale movements of auto racks, coal cars, grain cars, and chemical tank cars. Fortunately, vestiges of the good ol' days can still be found.

Unlike "mixed" freight trains of bygone eras, the current trend in railroad efficiency is yard-to-yard, non-stop single-commodity trains, **3, 4,** run as unit trains or large blocks of cars.

Let's start with what a railroad is not. Railroads are not in the entertainment business. A railroad doesn't design a track configuration because watching a train negotiate it would be interesting to watch, **5.** They don't add artificial complexity to add run time or to make switching moves challenging for crews. They don't do runaround moves because they are entertaining. They don't shuttle back and forth on switchback ladders for fun. Any real-world design engineer that took that approach would quickly be looking for new employment.

Improving speed and operational efficiency is an ongoing business priority. A prototype railroad will:
• Take the straightest/most economical route between two points (accounting for geography)
• Minimize runaround tracks

4

This auto-rack yard is an example of a single-commodity installation. Cars are loaded at auto plants and travel in solid trains or long cuts of cars to distribution yards like this one, where autos are transloaded to trucks for final delivery to dealers.

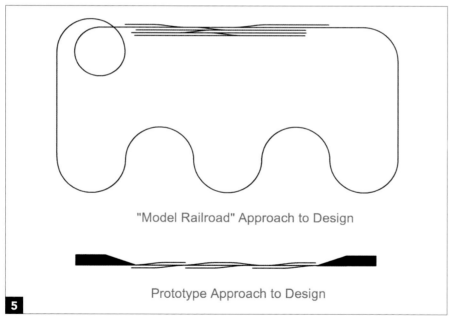

"Model Railroad" Approach to Design

Prototype Approach to Design

5

Model railroaders tend to approach design by running the main line in a way that creates the longest run. Prototype railroads look for the shortest option.

• Minimize switchbacks
• Rarely pick up a single car from one spot on a line, trundle 20 miles down the line and drop it at another business (a common feature of model railroad designs from the 1950s and 1960s)

Let's take a look at how railroads deal with some basic but real challenges associated with simply "moving around," given the fact they are limited to keeping things on the rails. Unlike airplanes, trucks, or ships, which are able to easily go up, down, or around each other, railroads don't have that luxury. They need special track arrangements to make it work, **6**.

Yards: We'll go into yards in much more detail in later chapters. At the most basic level, the purpose of a yard is to take incoming trains, break them down, organize (classify) the cars by final destination, and send them out again in an outgoing train, and do it expeditiously. Yards are *not* for storing cars—railroads make money by keeping cars moving.

Spurs: Spurs are single-ended tracks that serve as the originating and terminating point for cars switched to industries. Related to a train's direction of travel, spurs are referred to as "facing point" (track branches off ahead of the train) or "trailing point" (track branches off behind the train). More on those in a bit.

Interchanges: Interchange tracks connect competing railroads at junctions so they can exchange cars, and in some cases entire trains.

Sidings: Sidings serve two primary purposes. Passing sidings are designed for two trains to get around each other. The second function is for a locomotive to "run around" its train so it can go in the opposite direction. Some industrial tracks, especially those serving multiple businesses or very large ones, are double-ended. Let's look at sidings and spurs in more detail.

Sidings, spurs, and runarounds

A fast-moving truck on the interstate that encounters a slower moving vehicle simply moves to the left lane to make the pass. Even on a two-lane

Yard
1. Breaks down incoming trains
2. Classifies/sorts cars
3. Assembles trains

Siding
1. Allows trains to pass each other
2. Allows locomotives to move to the other end of a train

Industrial Spur
1. Allows businesses to load/unload cars
2. Can serve more than one industry

Interchange
Allows railroads to trade/exchange cars

6

Here are some common track arrangements used to accomplish a railroad's business objective.

road, the truck simply waits for a break in traffic and passes using the oncoming lane. For trains, it's much more of a challenge. On a single-track railroad the only option to avoid an oncoming train or pass a slower one is a passing siding, **7**.

Planning the number of sidings, their locations, and lengths is a major design decision. A double-track main line makes things much more efficient but at significantly higher infrastructure cost. Even then the problem isn't totally eliminated because trains going in the same direction may be traveling at different speeds.

Because of their cost and maintenance requirements, prototype railroads only place passing sidings where necessary, **8**. (Employee timetables list siding locations by milepost, usually with car capacity.) Sidings must be long enough to handle most trains on a given line (an issue

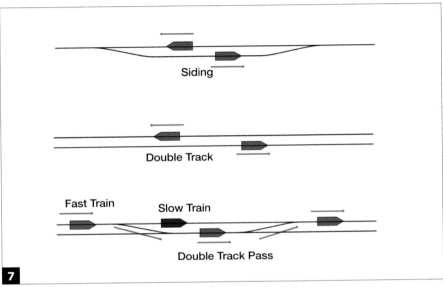

Siding

Double Track

Fast Train Slow Train

Double Track Pass

7

This sketch shows how on a single-track line, trains going in opposite directions or at different speeds use a siding to around each other (top). On a double-track line, crossovers are used for trains of varying speeds, to overtake (pass) each other (bottom).

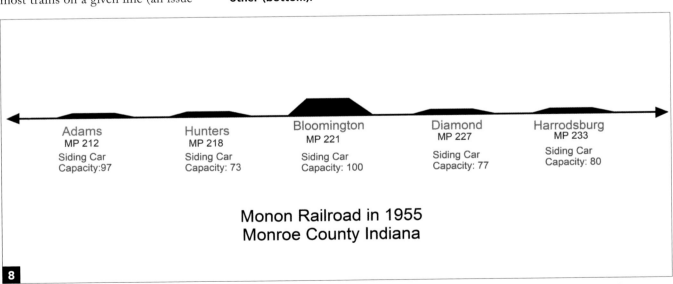

Adams MP 212	Hunters MP 218	Bloomington MP 221	Diamond MP 227	Harrodsburg MP 233
Siding Car Capacity:97	Siding Car Capacity: 73	Siding Car Capacity: 100	Siding Car Capacity: 77	Siding Car Capacity: 80

Monon Railroad in 1955
Monroe County Indiana

8

The location and distance between sidings has changed over time. This schematic of the Monon through Monroe County, Ind., in 1955 shows the spacing to be roughly every 4 or 5 miles. In modern times, with the ongoing trend toward less track, sidings are longer, fewer, and spaced much more widely.

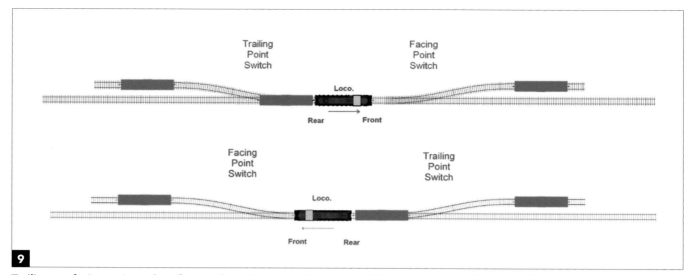

Trailing vs. facing point only refers to the orientation of a switch with respect to the direction a locomotive is traveling. In the top diagram, the switch on the left is trailing point, the one on the right is facing point. At bottom, with train direction reversed, the left switch is facing and the right one is trailing.

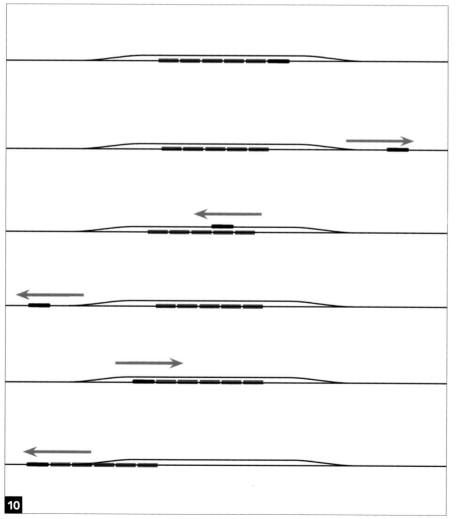

This illustrates a "runaround" move: using a double-ended siding to get the locomotive to the other end of the train. Prototype railroads do this to turn trains, but minimize runaround moves for switching purposes.

as train lengths increased in the 1960s and later). Busy main lines will have more sidings, spaced more closely together, than secondary or branch lines; sidings were more frequent (but shorter) in the steam era, when trains were typically shorter. Location is also an issue: As trains will be stopped on them, often for long periods of time, passing sidings rarely cross streets and highways at grade. They are often located just outside of towns, as opposed to running through them.

Before we discuss switching and runaround moves, it's important to understand the definition of facing-versus trailing-point switches, **9**. The orientation of a switch, whether it faces toward or away from an oncoming train, has major operational implications. Using the truck analogy again, if a truck pulls into a warehouse complex it doesn't matter whether the door it's looking for is on the left or right. For a railroad, any change in route has to be done through a switch, and the position of a switch relative to the direction a train is traveling is a key concept.

A facing-point switch is one where the points of the switch face the locomotive as it approaches it (the locomotive moving forward can pick either of two routes). A trailing-point switch is one where the points are behind the locomotive as it passes by (a reverse move can choose either route). Note that facing vs. trailing always refers to the position of the switch in relation to the direction of train movement—it has no respect to whether the switch is a left-hand, right-hand, or wye. A switch that is trailing point for an eastbound train is a facing point for a westbound. For a switching move you want the turnout to be trailing point so you can back in.

Runaround tracks are double-ended sidings that allow a locomotive to go around its train (or a car or group of cars) to get the train moving in the other direction, or to perform a switching move, such as to shove a car into a facing-point spur (more on those in a bit), **10**. Runaround moves are an entertaining operation ... for some model railroaders. On prototype

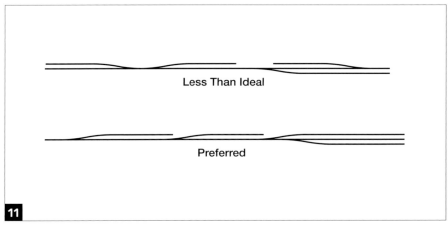

11

It is far more efficient to switch a group of spurs if all of the turnouts are facing in the same direction (lower), so that's the prototype's preferred arrangement from a design standpoint. When things are oriented this way, a train can easily switch cars out with simple push/pull moves without the need to run around a train to work switches facing in the opposite direction (top). That arrangement is much harder for a train to work, and prototype railroads try to avoid this format if they can.

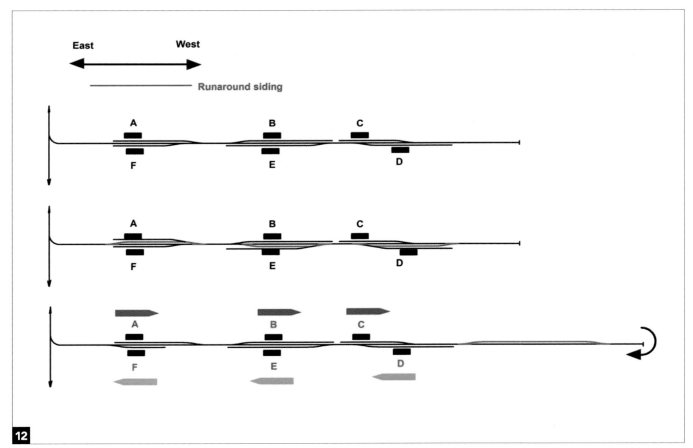

12

Here we have six industries, at three locations (or towns) on a branch line, each with turnouts facing in both directions. A typical "model railroad" approach to operating the line would be as in the middle diagram. A train leaving the junction at left would stop and work A and then the locomotive would run around its train so it could work F with the switch facing in the opposing direction. It would then work westward down the line doing the same at industries B and E and then C and D. A prototype railroad wouldn't do it that way. It would work down the line only working industries with trailing point switches at A, E, and C. It would then perform its only runaround move at the siding at the end of the line and return, working the trailing point switches at D, B, and F.

13

At first glance you might consider a spur, such as the one leading into Sweetener Products pictured above, to be one industry. However, corn syrup comes in different grades, with each car needing to be spotted at the proper hose to prevent contaminating the product. Each discharge hose is called a "car spot" or, in effect, a mini-industry.

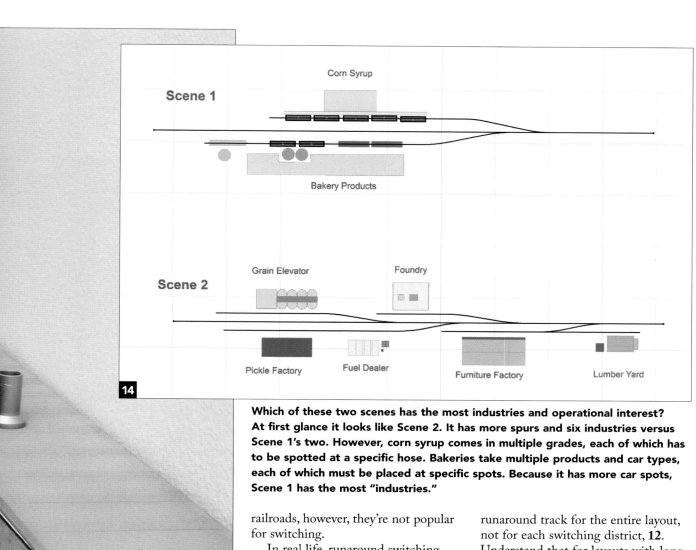

Scene 1

Corn Syrup

Bakery Products

Scene 2

Grain Elevator

Foundry

Pickle Factory

Fuel Dealer

Furniture Factory

Lumber Yard

14

Which of these two scenes has the most industries and operational interest? At first glance it looks like Scene 2. It has more spurs and six industries versus Scene 1's two. However, corn syrup comes in multiple grades, each of which has to be spotted at a specific hose. Bakeries take multiple products and car types, each of which must be placed at specific spots. Because it has more car spots, Scene 1 has the most "industries."

railroads, however, they're not popular for switching.

In real life, runaround switching moves are time consuming, expensive, dangerous, inefficient, and to be minimized or avoided if possible. Using a short double-ended industry track or dedicated runaround track is one thing, but using a mile-and-a-half long passing siding on a busy main line is another.

Although methods and rules vary by the railroad, situation, and individual conductors, on most mainline railroads a local freight will proceed down the line, switching all of the trailing point spurs along the way. Facing point switches are left for the return trip or for a separate train coming the other direction. A railroad would prefer that all stub-ended spurs face the same way, **11**, at least in any given area, but space often precludes this.

How does this impact layout design? For industrial switching or branch lines you really only need one runaround track for the entire layout, not for each switching district, **12**. Understand that for layouts with long main lines passing through multiple towns, the primary use of passing sidings is for trains to pass as opposed to doing switching runarounds.

Car spots

When planning the industries on a layout, one of the most important concepts to understand is that of a car spot. A car spot is a specific location within a given industry where a car must be placed. A single industry could have several car spots, each of which essentially equates to a mini-industry. By understanding this, we make operations more challenging and more realistic, reduce the number of necessary switches, and free up room for other elements.

Let's say that you have a food processor that receives flour and sugar (in covered hoppers), vegetable oil (in tank cars), and packaging and boxed products (in boxcars), **13**. As beginners we think of that food processor as one industry—it is not. The plant manager is not going to be happy if the flour is spotted by the tank car unloading pipe and the boxcar next to the hopper unloader. The plant needs the cars placed at specific "spots" next to the appropriate unloading equipment. When we break it down that way, our food processor actually contains three sub-industries, each car spot being that sub-industry. The switching potential of a layout therefore is not the number of industries but the number of car spots. You could very easily have a layout with only a few industries but dozens of car spots, **14**.

Defining and choosing industries

Freight trains move raw materials and products manufactured, mined, or otherwise created by industries. Modeling an industry's structures, rolling stock, and operations is one of the most interesting aspects of the hobby. Defining what an industry is, and picking the most appropriate ones for your situation, becomes a vital part of the design process. On the surface it would seem obvious: A coal mine is an industry, as is a factory that makes boxes. However, when you look deeper into a railroad's business model, there's a lot more depth to the subject—and with that, tremendous opportunities for modeling and operational interest.

Let's start by how we define an industry. An industry is *any* location where a car must be placed on the layout to serve a customer. The railroad itself can be the customer (a locomotive coaling station or ash pit, an interchange track with another railroad, etc.). Within a single customer compound there may be many individual and distinct locations—car spots—that receive cars. Each location becomes, in effect, a separate "mini-industry."

The industries you select for your layout will go a long way toward determining how operations actually play out. Depending on your approach to the hobby this could be a major design consideration. A key question to

15 A Florida East Coast Railway yard job works an aggregate loadout near Medley, Fla. The motive power (GP38-2/GP40-2) and rock will later head out on a unit train to Fort Pierce, Fla. *Tolga Erbora*

answer is how much, personally, do you care? Does it matter if your layout's overall look and operational scheme is plausible? If your enjoyment comes from simply building a variety of kits, you may be perfectly happy plopping that craftsman pickle factory next to an equally fun-to-build sawmill. If you are a casual "dump the car and go" operator, it may not matter either. If, however, operations and realism matter to you—or if you believe it will matter to you in the future—care needs to be given both in terms of a believable look and in selecting industries that spin off the most operational interest.

Several factors come into play when selecting industries to include on a layout. First is prototypical accuracy. If it's important to you to accurately model a specific place, then your choice is made for you whether it yields visual and operational interest or not (although you can sometimes pick and choose from multiple industries at any given location). If you have some

flexibility—if you're a proto-freelancer or freelancer, then you might want to give things a little more thought.

Some industries take up a lot of space but have very little going on operationally beyond long cuts of cars being shoved under a loader for eight hours a day. Common examples are modern grain elevators, modern coal mines, and aggregate facilities—these all often load entire trains at once.

However, other industries take a large variety of cars, and require that those cars be placed at specific spots. Given the choice, they make for better candidates for a model railroad. You can pack a lot more operational variety in a small amount of space and have the added bonus of car variety. Examples include paper mills, breweries, bakeries/food processors, corn syrup facilities, logistics/transloading warehouses, and steel mills. If I'm designing a freelanced layout for operation, I'll choose a paper mill over a modern coal mine 10 out of 10 times.

Let's break down industry types looking at them from a different viewpoint; specifically, their size, the variety of cars they receive, and the relationship between the two. Again, from an operational standpoint, a large industry that takes a lot of layout surface area, takes a single car type, and has minimal switching is less desirable. On the other side, an industry that receives a variety of car types, requires spot car placement, and takes up a modest amount of room is the most desirable.

Large industry/single commodity/one car type: coal (modern loader or power plant), grain elevator, aggregates, **15**, iron ore, phosphates. These facilities tend to be huge and take one type of car. Although they handle a tremendous amount of traffic (often more than 100 cars per day), switching moves tend to be basic and simple: movement often involves shoving long cuts of cars beneath a loader or unloader.

In this photo of Trujillo and Sons, a food products company in Miami, we can see boxcars (right), tank cars (left), and covered hoppers (far left) all spotted at specific unloading locations.

16

17

Pan Am Frozen food is a tiny rail-served french-fry company in Miami. It only takes one car type (refrigerator cars), but also doesn't take up much space and has an interesting look.

Even if an industry and its facilities or plant is fascinating to you, consider how the operations will relate to your layout. How would you like a crew job on a model railroad where you spend three solid hours shoving 150 phosphate cars through a loader at half a mile per hour?

Large industry/multiple car types/ multiple car spots: brewery, large food manufacturer/processor, **16**, steel mill, paper mill, logistics warehouse/ transloading center, chemical plant. The only downside to these from a modeling standpoint is that they take up a lot of space, but they provide a lot of operational interest per square foot. If you have the room, they are great candidates for a layout—they can even be the *entire* layout in some cases.

For example: A paper mill can receive boxcars of recycled paper, hoppers or gondolas of wood chips and/or flatcars or gondolas of pulpwood, and different types of tank cars for clay slurry and various

chemicals; it ships products in boxcars. A brewery can receive carloads of hops in insulated boxcars, malted barley in boxcars or covered hoppers, and tank cars of corn syrup. It can ship products out in refrigerator cars or insulated boxcars.

Modest-size industry/multiple car types/multiple car spots: corn syrup processors, small food processors, ethanol plants, small factories. These are the most efficient in terms of maximizing visual play value and operational play value per square foot. A classic example would be a food processor. They can be represented by a flat or half flat against a backdrop without taking too much space, and receive and ship a variety of cars, each of which need to be placed at a specific loading location (including boxcars for finished products, tank cars of vegetable oil, covered hoppers of grain,

flour, or sugar, and possibly plastic pellet hoppers for packaging machines".

Another good modern example is an ethanol plant, which receives corn in one type of covered hopper, ships out spent grain in another type of covered hopper, receives tank cars of gasoline (for denaturing), and ships out tank cars of ethanol.

Small industry/limited car types: fuel dealer, food wholesaler, **17**, lumber yard, feed mill, small manufacturing plant. This is typically the model railroad view of the world, and although small businesses that ship and receive single cars have evolved and become rare since the 1960s, they still exist. "Wallpaper" the layout with as many of these as you can. Taking the wallpaper approach does give you car variety and industry variety, but taken to an extreme it's not entirely plausible and can take on a caricaturish look. Handled with restraint it can be the source of a lot of fun. Examples are virtually limitless and include almost any type of small manufacturing or retail concern.

"Hidden" industries: These are things you wouldn't think of as industries per se, but they can include a variety of cars and operations. They include team tracks (where off-line industries can have cars spotted and load or unload them directly from trucks), **18**, interchange tracks, freight houses, and engine servicing spots (coaling towers, fueling stations). Interchange and team tracks in particular are great candidates for a layout in that they take up very little space and they take every conceivable type of car.

Plausibility

Even if you take operations and car variety out of the equation, plausibility/ believability still factors in. Those modeling a specific prototype have it easiest when it comes to industry selection: just model what's there, omitting and compressing as necessary. The freelance modeler faces the challenge of creating something plausible but without as much guidance. Even so, studying prototypes of areas similar to what you're modeling can take you a long way.

Era plays a big factor. Through the steam-to-diesel transition era and early diesel periods, specific patterns were followed. Most towns, even small ones, had one or more fuel (coal and oil) dealers, a lumber yard, a freight house, and team track (often adjacent to the depot). Almost every Midwestern and plains state town had one or more small grain elevators and a feed mill.

For the modern-era modeler with modest space, fewer options exist, but smaller industries can be found, such as plastics plants, LPG dealers, lumber yards, transload facilities, scrapyards/ recycling centers, and corn syrup transloaders.

Individual industries evolved significantly from the 1940s onward as well. For example, an Appalachian coal mine tipple in the steam or transition era may have four tracks for different

grades of coal (requiring multiple spots for empties, with cars bound for multiple destinations), and load 15 or 20 cars per day. Today, a large mine loadout will load 120 identical cars at once bound for a single power plant.

Keep these factors in mind regarding prototype railroads and industries:

- Railroads are in the efficiency business, not the entertainment business. Prototype railroads use the least amount of track and fewest turnouts to get the job done. Track arrangements and operations will be laid out in a manner to get things accomplished as quickly and safely as possible.

- Prototype railroads prefer to have all industrial turnout spurs facing the same direction to avoid runaround moves. Especially on busy main lines, they will switch opposing-point turnouts with separate trains from each direction. Branch and other lines often have local freights operate as "turns" (out-and-back) so they can switch opposing turnouts on the return trip.

- Switchbacks are avoided if at all possible. Stacked switchbacks are a virtual never (legendary modeler John Allen's "timesaver" switching design, although fun as a puzzle, would never be designed in the real world).

- If you get stuck on how to handle the design of a specific track arrangement, looking at prototype railroad maps/diagrams and copying what they do provides a concrete example. Even if it's not of your exact prototype, they can serve as a realistic guide.

- Regardless of their size, industries that receive and ship out a variety of products provide more "entertainment" value per square foot than single-commodity businesses.

- Industry "spots" are essentially mini-businesses in and of themselves and create more operational play value per square foot than a collection of individual industries.

18 At team tracks almost any car type can be spotted. The top photo shows a spur in Miami, where a lumber car is being unloaded and tank cars await unloading. At left is a similar example next to New York New Jersey Rail's Bay Ridge (65th Street) Yard, with many goods stored on the ground.

CHAPTER THREE

Basic design tools

How various types of track, grades, and negative space impact layout design

CSX intermodal train Q031 illustrates the linear nature of railroads as it ducks under the Halifax Road bridge near Collier Yard in Petersburg, Va.
Tolga Erbora

At this point in the journey we should now have some of our more important decisions in hand in terms of what we want to accomplish strategically. The next step is coming up with a vehicle to execute that strategy ... the "design." As a starting point we need to have an understanding of the tools we have to work with. Some might seem obvious; others, not so much.

First, let's take a look at the individual components (design tools) we have to work with (we'll discuss their use in combination in the next chapter). These include straight track sections, curved track, turnouts, and crossings, as well as grades (changes in elevation), backdrops, and the use of negative space. How we use each of these tools impacts overall layout design, so understanding each of them in depth will pay off when we start putting everything together.

Straight (tangent) track

Straight track? Linear runs? We're going to talk about that? Granted, the concept of "straight track" at first seems so obvious and basic that it's easy to wonder why it even merits discussion. The reason is that it's crucial to recognize the importance of linear elements and make them a priority in our layout designs.

Why the emphasis? The main reason is that we are modeling or copying a subject—prototype railroads and their surroundings—that is, for the most part, linear, **1**. If we want to have a reasonable facsimile in model form we need to follow suit. Railroads are keenly aware that their focus isn't transportation, it's making money. The fastest, shortest, and therefore cheapest way to get from point A to point B is almost always a straight line (geographic obstacles being the exception).

Railroads don't string together multiple reverse curves across a cornfield because of aesthetics, or because they think it would be cool to watch a train wind around them. On prototype railroads, curves cause excess flange wear on wheels and additional wear on railheads. Curves impart additional drag (which uses more fuel and requires more power to overcome), especially on grades, and add operational headaches such as speed restrictions, car length/load restrictions, visibility issues, and other complications. Railroads avoid curves whenever possible.

Because of this, from a modeling standpoint linear runs are not only the most realistic, they are the most

Always test curves with your most troublesome cars. These HO 90-foot passenger cars are underweight and have diaphragms and short coupler shanks. The manufacturer claims a 24" minimum radius (not even close!); here they are barely making it through a 31.5" curve. Note the overhang on the car at right.

On a 34" curve the cars skim through without complaint. For HO, I've found 34" safe for the vast majority of cars on the market. There's still overhang, but not as much as on the tighter curve.

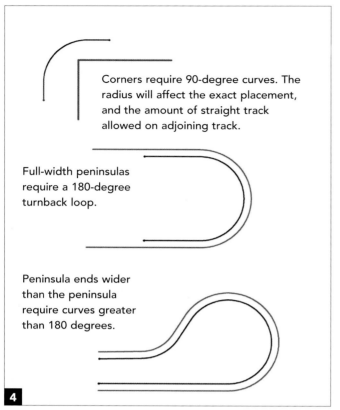

Corners require 90-degree curves. The radius will affect the exact placement, and the amount of straight track allowed on adjoining track.

Full-width peninsulas require a 180-degree turnback loop.

Peninsula ends wider than the peninsula require curves greater than 180 degrees.

4

The two most common locations you'll need to employ a curve are at a corner (top) and at the end of peninsula (middle and bottom).

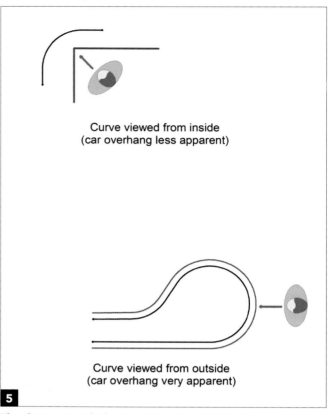

Curve viewed from inside (car overhang less apparent)

Curve viewed from outside (car overhang very apparent)

5

The degree to which unsightly car overhang becomes an issue depends upon whether you view the curve from the inside (where overhang is not so apparent) or the outside (where it's very apparent).

operationally reliable and easiest to deal with in terms of blending turnouts and lineside industries seamlessly into a design—far more than fighting to get the geometry to work for placing the same element on a curve (curved turnouts are available, but are expensive and can be an operational challenge). The more straight runs we have in our design and the fewer curves, the more efficient and realistic the plan. Of course, that is in a "perfect world," a world we don't live in.

Unlike prototype railroads, which in many areas of the country have the luxury of going tens of miles with no curves (or just small ones), we have to deal with the reality of room walls or peninsula ends that inconveniently crop up every 10 or 20 feet. We have the challenge of trying to represent what stretches out and transpires over tens of miles, then twist and bend it into ridiculously small amounts of space and do so in a way that looks passably realistic and operates reliably.

Which brings us to ... the "dreaded" need for curves.

Curved track

Especially in non-mountainous areas, prototype railroads have the luxury of running arrow straight for miles. We modelers don't have that same luxury. No matter how large our basements, in rather short order we'll hit the literal wall and need to turn either left, right, or completely around and go in the other direction.

As the late John Armstrong—the hobby's noted layout-design guru—frequently wrote, curves (including their radius and placement) can be a driving factor in many (but not all) designs. This was even more of an issue with the design styles that typified his era from the 1950s through the 1970s. It's important to understand curves' importance, the factors that make them important, the situations where their treatment is important, and situations where it is less so. For now I'm going

to temporarily put aside the aesthetic value of curves and S-curves. We'll deal with them later.

Curves serve two purposes on a model railroad: to make a 90-degree bend to avoid an upcoming wall or to make a 180-degree turn at the end of a peninsula. Curves are defined by their radius. In working with them, we need to consider two factors: visual appearance and the mechanical ability of rolling stock to negotiate a specific radius.

Appearance largely depends on whether you are looking at the curve from the inside, such as facing a 90-degree curve in a corner, or the outside, such as on the end of peninsula. The primary visual consideration is avoiding the dreaded, toy-like appearance of excess car overhang seen when a train (particularly with longer cars) negotiates tight curves. When viewed from the inside of a curve this overhang isn't as noticeable; when

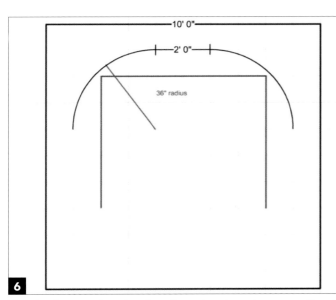
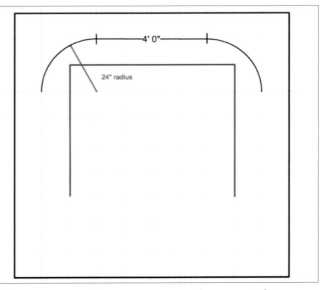

6 Here's what you lose by choosing a too-broad curve radius. Since these curves are in corners, car overhang won't be as apparent, allowing us to choose the minimum needed mechanically. At right, a 24" radius allows a 4-foot connecting tangent run; increasing radius to 36" (left) drops the straight segment to just 2 feet.

viewed from the outside, it is very much apparent.

Minimum radius

Selecting a minimum radius for your layout is a crucial design decision. If you guess too small you'll quickly get a demonstration of what a "clothesline" or "stringline" derailment looks like. Guess too large and you could end up wasting vital space. For the purposes of this section when I refer to "minimum" I'm referring to the mechanical aspect, not the visual. We are looking for a minimum radius where the rolling stock we expect to use will track reliably using a broad range of locomotives and cars. We aren't talking bare minimum—we're talking "comfortable" minimum, something with a bit of cushion worked in.

I divide rolling stock into two categories:

Category one: four-axle diesels, 40- to 60-foot freight cars, and short (three driving axle) steam locomotives. Since this category covers all of my personal layouts and is the most common with my clients, I've tested it extensively. Without question the number is 24" in HO scale (12" in N and 43" in O scale). A radius of this size will easily handle the rolling stock just described.

Category two: Here's where it gets dicey because there are a lot

more variables. This includes: six-axle diesels, 90-foot freight cars (auto racks, auto-parts cars, and piggyback flats), and 90-foot passenger cars. The extra variables? Steam vs. Diesel. Long-wheelbase steam locomotives (four or more driving axles)—especially brass imports—will have a lot harder time negotiating a tight curve than an SD40 with its swiveling trucks. Passenger cars add additional variables: do they have four or six axles? Long- or short-shank couplers (body or truck mounted)? And—a crucial element—do they have diaphragms (a nice detail that will quickly send your prize train to the bottom of the canyon if you go too tight on the curves)? For category two I set the "safe" minimum radius in HO at 34" (17" in N, 60" in O).

Is this overly conservative? Perhaps, and you might be able to comfortably and safely drop that down. But be aware that manufacturers' recommendations on minimum curves tend to be, to put it politely, extremely optimistic. The only way to know for sure with category two rolling stock is to do a mock-up of the curves on the floor or a table and run tests with the specific equipment you plan to use, **2, 3**. Run equipment by pulling and pushing and at slow and high speeds.

If your plan has a center peninsula, the minimum radius will be a driving

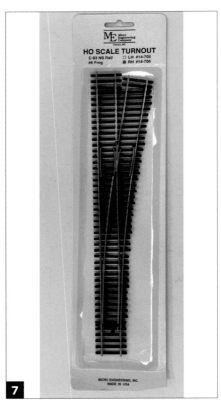

7 The basic act of moving from one track to another seems simple enough. Mechanically it's handled by a device called a turnout or switch (in this case, a Micro-Engineering no. 6). Turnouts (including their size and how many to include) are primary considerations in terms of how we design our layouts, so we need to understand all of the factors related to them.

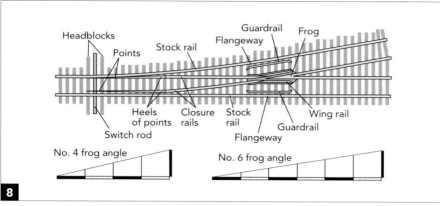

8

Turnouts are measured by the angle of the diverging track: The lower the number, the sharper the angle. Sharper turnouts (nos. 4 and 5) save space, but can create mechanical reliability issues, particularly with longer rolling stock. Broader turnouts (no. 8 and above) look fantastic and are very reliable, but they take up a lot of room. A good compromise is the no. 6.

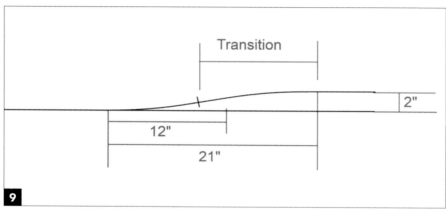

9

A typical no. 6 turnout in HO is almost a foot long. However, that's not the full story: Depending on the location, many turnouts will also need transitions into and out of them. The amount of space you need to allocate for a typical siding turnout is 21".

When sketching trackwork, turnouts—especially yard ladders—are notorious for being greatly compressed. In this example, what was sketched at 22" actually takes up twice as much length when drawn to scale.

10

factor in the design and how much you can fit into your space, **4**. With the more recent trend toward more-linear, shelf-style formats with *no* center peninsula, curves play a much less-crucial role in terms of how much they drive a design. We will talk a number of times about how critical the decision is as to whether to incorporate a peninsula with turn-back curve on it, and now we enter the technical reasons as to how that plays out.

Complicating things is that when we look at mechanical reliability, we can't just look at the curve in isolation—we need to understand the impact of what's on each side of it and how we transition into and out of those neighboring elements, specifically turnouts.

Also, with a center peninsula it's not just the diameter of the curve that eats up a tremendous amount of space. We must also factor in a minimum 2"-3" scenery buffer between the curve and layout fascia. We'll discuss this in more detail in the next chapter.

A note on visual appearance: Many ask if a curve isn't visible, if a larger radius than the minimum is needed for mechanical reliability? The answer is no, anything more is a waste of our all too limited space. If you're viewing from the inside of a curve you can get away with much tighter curves, **5**. If however, the curve will be viewed from the outside, as on a peninsula, then aesthetics start playing a role and you'll need to make your own decisions in terms of what you can live with, where you strike a balance in terms of how much you want to increase the radius over the minimum to increase appearance.

Also remember that increasing curve radius in corners is often possible, **6**, but will significantly reduce the length of straight track between corners.

Turnouts

Turnouts, **7**, are critical track components, allowing us to have changes in route as well as sidings, spurs, and yards. They are labeled as left- or right-hand, depending upon which way the diverging track branches from the straight route. Wye turnouts have both routes diverging from the straight path.

Turnouts come in various sizes, indicated by numbers: The smaller the number, the sharper the angle of the diverging track, **8**. The number is the length-to-width ratio of the diverging route to the main route (this applies regardless of modeling scale). For example, a no. 6 turnout takes 6" of run to separate 1". Commercial turnouts are made in many sizes, with nos. 4, 5, 6, and 8 the most common. Numbers 4 and 5 are considered sharp, 6 medium, and 8 broad.

When planning a layout it's crucial to understand how much space each turnout takes up. It's a lot more than you'd expect: More than one modeler has fallen into the trap of finding out that their pencil sketches of a track plan aren't buildable because the turnouts weren't drawn to scale. As an example, an HO no. 6 turnout is almost a foot long, but adding transition trackage to get parallel track separation (or separation from neighboring curves) significantly stretches the distance it takes up, **9**.

Even when the designer is clear on the geometric issues, other factors come into play. First is cost. Depending on how you plan to control turnouts, you may also have expenses related to switch machines, control linkage, toggle switches, stationary decoders, control panels, and a separate power supply and other wiring.

Second is maintenance. If you have a mechanical or electrical malfunction on your layout (derailment, short circuit, dead spot, or other wiring issue), nine times out of ten it will be at—you guessed it—a turnout!

The takeaway from all of this is to avoid sprinkling turnouts over your design like pepper on a steak. Use them sparingly and only when they provide a very clear design and operational benefit. Prototype railroads avoid them when possible (especially on main tracks) for similar reasons. An ongoing point of this book is that one the measuring sticks of layout complexity is turnout count.

Because of the back and forth

11 Yard ladders take up a lot of space, but laying out actual components to see the actual size will give you more accurate feel for their appearance than just a drawing. Trying to use too-sharp turnouts will result in less-dependable operation.
Andy Sperandeo

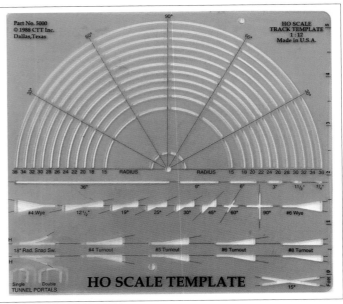

12 If you're going to hand-sketch your design, track-drawing templates can help insure that your turnouts are drawn to actual scale.

13 The vacant parking lot on my HO scale CSX East Rail layout is an example of negative space used in an urban environment.

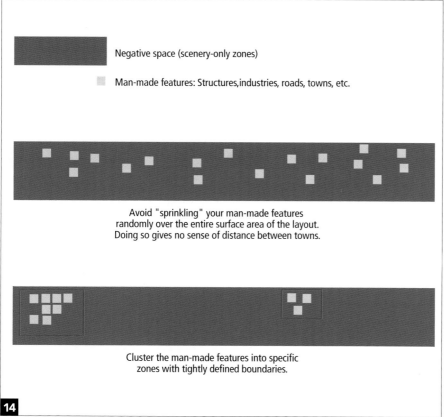

Negative space (scenery-only zones)

Man-made features: Structures, industries, roads, towns, etc.

Avoid "sprinkling" your man-made features randomly over the entire surface area of the layout. Doing so gives no sense of distance between towns.

Cluster the man-made features into specific zones with tightly defined boundaries.

14 Effective application of negative space entails clustering manmade features into specific zones with ample space separating them. Avoid indiscriminately "wallpapering" the surface of your layout with manmade features, particularly if they have no plausible relationship to one another.

movement and jarring a train experiences when passing through a turnout, planning consideration needs to be given to how you transition into and out of them and what other track features you place at the entry and exit points (especially curves and grades). If you aren't careful, you run the risk of derailments. Good general rules are to allow 4"-6" between the end of a curve and the beginning of a turnout, and to keep turnouts 6"-9" away from the top and bottom of grades.

Turnout count warrants a really hard and close look. Because of the natural tendency to include too many in a design, you need to watch the number closely if it starts marching upward. A clean, well-designed plan follows the lead of prototype railroads and employs the absolute fewest to get the job done.

Turnout optimism

Model railroaders are an optimistic bunch, particularly when it comes to layout design! But, as noted earlier, we tend to be overly optimistic when it comes to sketching turnout geometry, **10**. We all do quick sketches to illustrate a point or figure out details of

15 The large field on my N scale Monon layout shows an example of negative space used in a rural setting.

a track plan. Trouble looms, however, when we stay with the "quick sketch" approach as we delve more deeply into developing a design.

When customers send me sketches of a concept they have in mind, almost to a person, the turnouts are drawn to dimensions that don't exist in the real world. The problem is that turnouts, when drawn to scale, are much, much larger than we would think. The issue compounds itself when you combine multiple switches in a complex track arrangement such as a yard ladder, **11**. If you get too far ahead of yourself using a sketched design with grossly non-scale turnouts as placeholders, eventually you'll be hit with the cold hard truth that what you had in mind simply won't fit.

The first step is to realize the potential problem early on. Next, move as quickly as possible to using templates of scale turnouts when doing your sketches, **12**. I try to stick to a minimum "best practice" of nothing sharper than a no. 6 turnout.

Negative space

"The area around the primary objects in a work of art is known as negative space, while the space occupied by the primary objects is known as positive space."— *J. Paul Getty museum*

"Negative space" in a model railroad plan can be a difficult concept to wrap your mind around initially— "nothingness" as a design element sounds odd. However, it's a critical idea to embrace if you want to create the distinction between a "model of a railroad" and a "toy train set." Negative space is one of the most significant contributors to an effective design, **13**. To be specific, I'm referring primarily to the empty space between elements. Not only does negative space apply to separating scenes, it also applies to allowing space between elements within a scene—two structures, for example.

It's a subject many modelers struggle with as they face the challenge of having a long list of "must-have elements" competing for limited benchwork space. There's also a tendency to spread these elements evenly across a scene, when they should often be grouped together—groups of structures, for example, **14**. Failing to recognize and embrace the importance of negative space is the leading culprit in missing the mark visually, resulting

in a lack of realism and failure to capture the essence of a time and place.

Prototype railroads go from one place to the next. In order to create the illusion on a layout that A and B are in fact two different places, we need some space between them, **15**. Every day of our lives we exist in the real world of geography and scenery and urban landscape. We have an innate sense of how far apart things actually are in the real world. If we push those limits, then plausibility suffers. So, yes, empty space is every bit as important (if not more) as a depot, grain elevator, town, or yard.

When you think of negative space in those terms and give it its rightful place in the hierarchy, you'll see a dramatic improvement in the visual balance (and perhaps mechanical reliability) of your designs, **16**. Instead of thinking "the depot goes here, the road here," train yourself to think "the empty space goes here and here, the depot over there."

In the railroad environment, examples of negative space include any open area devoid of structures or three-dimensional man-made elements. Examples include fields, parking lots,

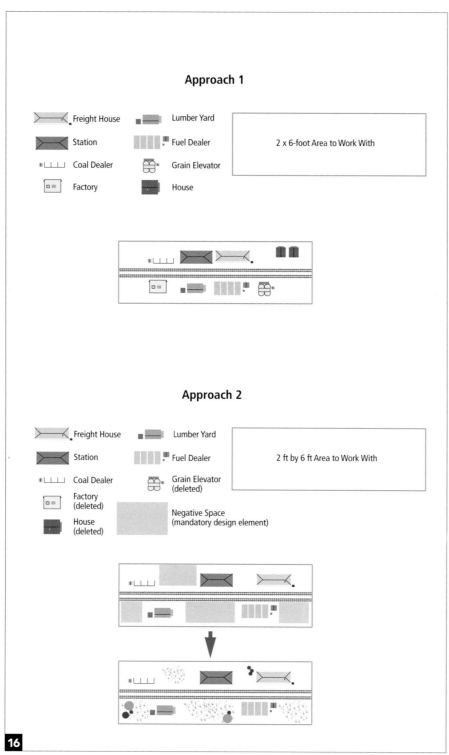

Approach 1

Freight House

Station

Coal Dealer

Factory

Lumber Yard

Fuel Dealer

Grain Elevator

House

2 x 6-foot Area to Work With

Approach 2

Freight House

Station

Coal Dealer

Factory
(deleted)

House
(deleted)

Lumber Yard

Fuel Dealer

Grain Elevator
(deleted)

Negative Space
(mandatory design element)

2 ft by 6 ft Area to Work With

16

Let's look at using negative space to handle a typical scene composition. In Approach 1, we have a scene we'd like to fit in a 2x6-foot area. At upper left of the diagram are a lot of must-have structures we'd like to incorporate. Space is tight so we squeeze them closely together and eliminate almost all negative space. The end result will look like a toy, not a model of a railroad. In Approach 2, negative space is added as a must-have design element. Not only is it an element, it's treated as a top priority. To make room for it, the decision is made to eliminate some of the structures to make room for the negative space. The resulting scene becomes much more balanced and realistic.

17

vacant lots, **17**, forested and wooded areas, and other non-descript "scenery-only" zones.

Grades

On prototype railroads, the purpose of grades—any track that isn't level—is to gain or lose elevation, which usually means to traverse a natural landform (hill, valley, or mountain) or get over or under a manmade element such as another railroad or roadway, **18**, **19**. On a layout, grades can serve several purposes, **20**. One is operational interest. Having a slope steep enough for a train to require pushers or helpers can introduce a fascinating operating scenario. Just as with the prototype, they can be used on our layouts to get over tracks or a street.

My design customers also often ask to have them included in a design for

Veteran modeler Clark Propst is known for his scene composition skills. Note the realism achieved by inserting this vacant lot (negative space) behind the team track and platform. *Clark Propst*

Prototype railroads rise or fall in elevation for man-made features, such as this underpass along the Illinois Terminal south of Mackinaw Junction, Ill., in 1970. *Mike Schafer*

Prototype railroads also use grades to conquer nature, as with this Conrail train on Washington Hill in western Massachusetts in 1978. *Leigh F. Savoye*

On my N scale Monon layout I wanted to capture the prototype pusher grade north out of Bloomington to the siding at Hunters. The prototype was roughly 1.7 percent, and I set the layout grade the same. With three F units, some curves, and weighted cars, when the train length hit about 20 cars the train stalled and I needed pushers on the rear end. *Paul Dolkos*

another reason: they think it will add visual interest. I caution them against that if this is the goal. Grades gentle enough that our trains can easily climb them generally aren't as visually noticeable as you'd expect. If visual interest (not operational) is the goal, I generally suggest accomplishing the sense of vertical distance through the use of scenery such as hills, mountains, and downward dropping ravines as opposed to sloping the track.

Calculating grades

Grades are expressed as a percentage. To determine a grade, divide the amount of the rise by the amount of the run. For example, if elevation rises 1" over 100" of track length, it's 1÷100, which equals .01 or 1 percent. An inch of elevation rise over 75" of run would be 1÷75=.013, or 1.3 percent, and so on.

Regardless for your reason for incorporating a grade, there's no free lunch. Grades take longer to build than flat roadbed. In addition they add physical constraints in terms of limiting train length, and if not installed correctly in the vertical plane, they increase the potential for derailments (especially at turnouts on grades).

Prototype railroads avoid grades and hills whenever possible (often limiting or eliminating them at great cost) because of these operational issues. This is another case where following the prototype's lead and avoiding unnecessary grades will pay off in operational reliability.

When including grades you need to pay close attention to gradient percentage, **21** (grade calculations are the same regardless of scale). If the slope is too steep, trains won't be able to climb the hill. As with turnouts, it's easy when doing rough

sketches to compress things and make grades impossibly steep. It's difficult to provide guidelines for a specific maximum grade when designing a layout because there are so many variables in play.

What your locomotives can actually pull on a specific hill will be determined by the locomotive type, length of the slope, curvature (curves add drag), number of cars in a typical train, the weight of the cars, and how free-rolling your trucks/wheels are. Some locomotives—particularly steam locomotives in N scale and small steam locomotives and many older imported brass steam locomotives in HO—are notoriously weak pullers on grades.

I surveyed several of my friends regarding grades, and the range of maximum gradients they used was extreme. For our purposes I suggest approaching any grades steeper than 1.75 percent with caution. The acid test is to assemble a mockup with a

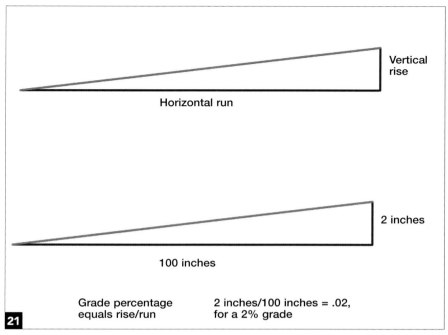

21

Grades are numbered as a percentage: rise over run. For example, a track that rises 2" in elevation over 100" length of track is a 2 percent grade (2÷100=.02).

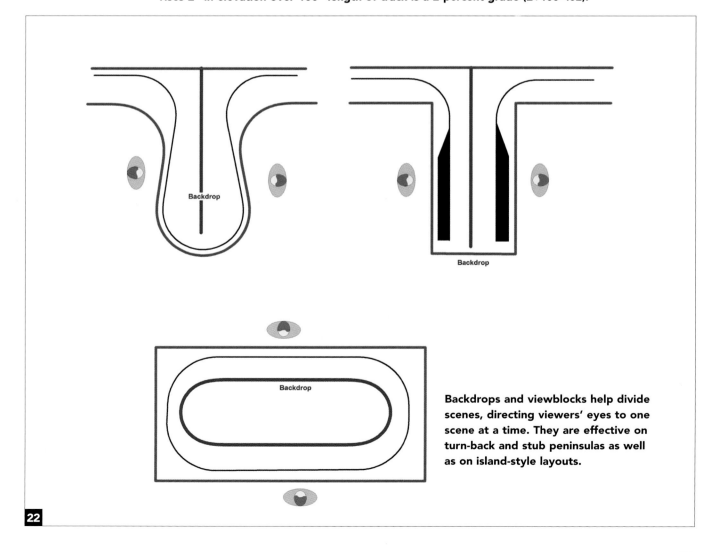

22

Backdrops and viewblocks help divide scenes, directing viewers' eyes to one scene at a time. They are effective on turn-back and stub peninsulas as well as on island-style layouts.

23 The backdrop splits the benchwork on this peninsula. Backdrops can vary in height based on benchwork height, ceiling height, access to hidden track, and other variables.

24 The backdrop can be rounded at the end of a peninsula. Here a double-track turnback loop doubles back around the end of the backdrop, hidden from the scene at left.

track on a slope (long enough to hold an entire train) and perform a trial run with the actual locomotives and rolling stock you plan to use.

Keep in mind if you need to gain elevation with grades on main lines that contain features such as yards, industrial spurs, and most sidings, they need to remain level. And with today's free-rolling wheelsets and trucks, you'll quickly discover any track that isn't level.

Another key is that what goes up has to come down. If you have a continuous-run layout and you add a grade going up, you'll need the main line to come back down to elevation zero to close the loop vertically. That means that, all things being equal, you can only gain half as much height as you'd be able to on a point-to-point layout where you don't have to worry about getting back down. This can be a serious consideration if you're modeling a stretch of mountainous railroad.

Be aware of clearance requirements wherever one track crosses over another. Be sure to account for the size of the lower portions of a bridge, as well as the height of the roadbed, subroadbed, and the track structure (rails and ties) on the lower track. Run tests with your tallest locomotives and freight cars, and add a scale foot or two of additional clearance.

Here's a summary of key considerations regarding grades:
- Longer grades create more drag then shorter ones
- Curves create more drag on grades than straight track
- Yards, spur tracks, and sidings need to be level
- Grades shouldn't start or end abruptly: the track should ease into and out of the top and bottom of each grade
- Acceptable grades will vary depending upon locomotive type, car weight, train length, and rolling characteristics of rolling stock
- Grades shouldn't be added merely for visual effect

Backdrops and view blocks
Controlling the line of sight is a vital part of layout design. By judiciously

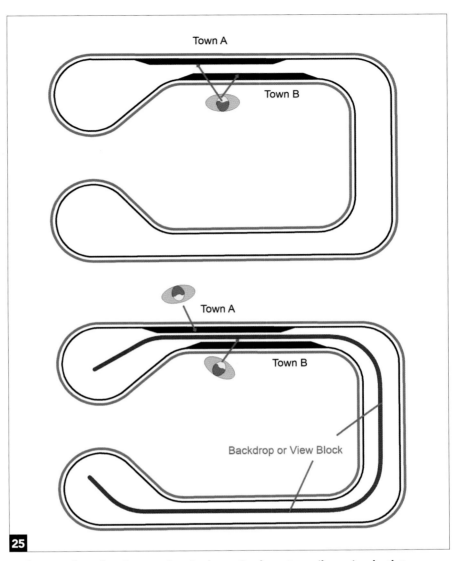

25

In the top plan, the viewer takes in the entire layout, easily seeing both town A and town B. This destroys the sense of distance and makes the layout appear smaller. In the bottom, the backdrop controls what the viewer can see— preventing seeing A and town B at the same time. This enhances the sense of distance and space.

guiding what the eye can see—and artfully blocking what it cannot—we can make a layout look much larger and more realistic. When we talk about backdrops, generally the first thing that comes to mind is the visual or artistic aspect. While suggesting atmosphere and distance is important, for design purposes backdrops can take on an equally important role as a view block. By placing them judiciously they can separate scenes and create a much needed sense of distance, **22**.

This can be especially effective for peninsulas (short or long and serpentine), **23**, **24**. Without a backdrop the eye takes in the entire scene across the benchwork, making it appear as one distinct geographic location. By dividing the scene with the backdrop it separates them, doubling the apparent space, **25**. Island-style layouts especially benefit from this.

CHAPTER FOUR

Combining track elements

Blending components to create sidings, spurs, yards, and other features

A CSX locomotive shoves a cut of cars into an industrial spur to make a setout. Spurs are a basic building block of layout and track plan design.
Tolga Erbora

Now that we understand the trackwork components and features (tools) we have available to us as individual parts, let's move to the next step, which is understanding how they are combined to serve the underlying purpose of moving freight over the line, **1**. We'll look at basics of sidings, spurs, and other trackwork, and see the purposes served by various types of yards.

We'll also look at crossings, double-track configurations, transition tracks, wyes, and special installations such as engine servicing areas. We'll then examine "best practices"—establishing a minimum radius for curves and minimum turnout size, and determining track center distances, reach-in distances, benchwork width, and other dimensions crucial to layout design.

Spurs and sidings

Just as the turnout is the basic piece of track that allows us to create varying routes and features, spurs and sidings are the basic building blocks we'll add to the mainline route, **2**. A spur is a single-ended track diverging from the main or another track; it terminates at a bumper or other type of rail stop. Spurs are typically used to serve industries; multiple spurs can branch off like roots on a tree to serve multiple industries or multiple spots at the same industry (we'll go into more detail on them in Chapter 7).

Sidings are double-ended (a turnout at each end) and parallel to the main track. Their main purpose is to allow trains to pass each other; they also allow locomotives to run around their trains during switching maneuvers. Some industrial tracks are double-ended; these may serve multiple businesses, or have additional spur tracks coming off of them.

Passing sidings are, ideally, long enough to hold one train, **3**. You'll need to have an idea of your future operating scheme when determining this. Be sure to include locomotive length (including multiple diesels) and a caboose if applicable. Passing sidings often need to be much longer than many modelers initially allow for— even a fairly short transition-era train of a dozen 50-foot cars, a caboose, and two F units in HO is about 9 feet long. Add another foot at each end to allow for turnouts, and you have an 11-foot stretch of track. Runaround tracks can be shorter (more on those in Chapter 7 as well).

Typical towns and industrial areas combine spurs and runaround tracks in various arrangements, **4**.

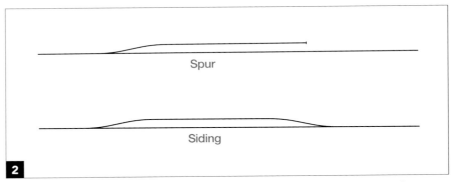

2

A spur (top) is when one track splits into two and the branch terminates in a stub. A siding (bottom) is when one track splits into two and then transitions back to one again. Sidings allow trains to pass one another and locomotives to run around their trains.

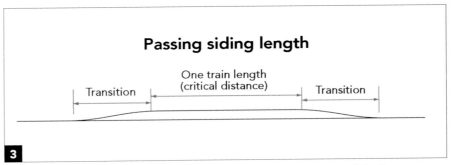

3

The length of a passing siding ideally is one train length. Be careful where you take this measurement: It should be the length of the siding where the train is totally in the clear and not fouling the main line. When calculating train length, be sure to allow for the caboose and multiple locomotives if applicable.

4

Corning, Iowa, on the Burlington had two crossovers, a double-ended industry track (left), and a spur behind the depot to the elevator. *Henry J. McCord*

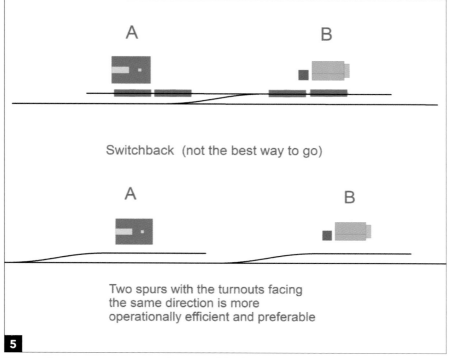

Switchback (not the best way to go)

Two spurs with the turnouts facing the same direction is more operationally efficient and preferable

5

The track arrangement at top is a switchback. In order to switch the cars at A, a switcher has to first remove the cars at B, then switch A, and finally put the cars back at B. This is very inefficient. Although commonly used by novice layout designers, for the most part prototype railroads use them only if absolutely necessary, and will opt for separate spurs (bottom) when possible.

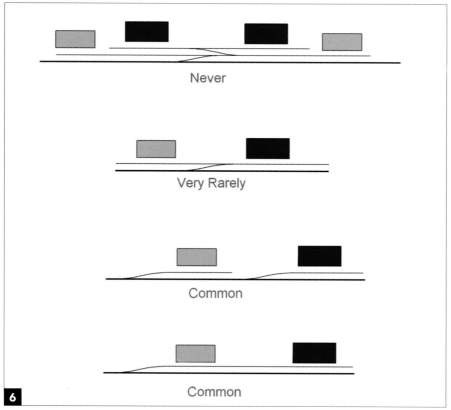

Never

Very Rarely

Common

Common

6

The stacked multi-switchback at top—which are found too often in track plans—aren't prototypical and should be avoided, and individual spurs substituted.

Switchbacks

A switchback refers to a track orientation where a spur splits off from another spur, but in the opposite direction, **5**. Switchbacks are often used by novice designers as a space-saving technique in industrial areas with multiple customers. The problem is that during operations, when you try to switch the spurs (particularly if both leads are packed with cars), you quickly realize how ungainly and inefficient they are. If both leads are full, one industry's tracks must be pulled and cleared before you can gain access to the needed track. You then need to switch the cars back.

Switchbacks do occur in the real world, but be aware that prototype railroads avoid them whenever possible because of these problems. Don't fall into the common model railroad design trap of adding switchbacks to increase operational interest, **6**—there are other ways to do that, as we'll discuss throughout the coming chapters.

Crossings and interchange tracks

Crossings are simple tracks that allow two routes to intersect at grade, without a connection that allows trains to move from one route to another, **7, 8**. Their most common use on prototype railroads is allowing competing railroads (or multiple routes of one railroad) to cross, **9**. They can also be found in industrial areas, especially where clearances are tight. They are measured by their intersecting angle in degrees, with prefab model track commonly available in 90-, 60-, 45-, and 30-degree angles.

Interchange tracks allow trains at crossings to pass from one route to another, with a turnout on each route linked by a connector track, **10**. Multiple or longer tracks can be used at busy crossings. These tracks are typically used to exchange cars between railroads; in some operations, entire trains may pass between routes. We can simulate these on model railroads in partial form by modeling just the turnout on our modeled line, running the interchange off the front

7

8

Grade crossings can be simple, with one line crossing another, or complex, like this one, with multi-track main lines intersecting. *Linn H. Westcott*

Crossings can be found in and around yards and industrial areas, wherever space is tight. *TRAINS magazine collection*

9

10

Crossings are measured by the angle at which the tracks intersect. On layouts, they are often used as an aesthetic or scenic feature. Crossings are relatively easy to incorporate into a design with minimal impact.

David Gallaway's HO layout has a crossing with an interchange track that disappears as it angles back to the backdrop and behind a hill. The foreground track is a dummy; it ends at the edge of the fascia. *David Gallaway*

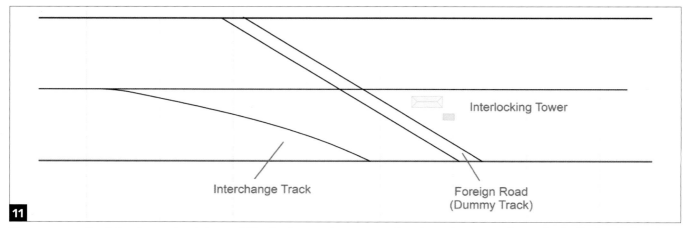

11

You can run a live interchange track toward the fascia at a dummy crossing. Interchange tracks are basically free industries, plus the bonus that interchange tracks can take almost any type of car.

12

CSX's double-track main (at left) passes the Washington Post facility outside of College Park, Md. The Metro system to the right is also double-tracked. Note the short double-ended siding with spur heading into the Post building.

of the layout, **11**, or into the backdrop. This lets us use the interchange track to set out and pick up cars during operations even if we don't have room to model the other main line.

Double-track main lines

Prototype railroads sometimes opt for two main tracks instead of one, to ease congestion on routes that see especially heavy traffic, **12**. Some of the most-famous and popular prototype routes have double track, but be aware that multi-track routes are actually rather

rare in the real world. They involve a vast additional expense, including the second track itself (including roadbed and extra right-of-way width), double the number of bridges (or wider, more-expensive bridges), additional signal installations and complexity, and increased maintenance costs.

There are typically two reasons modelers want a double-track main line for their layout. One is modeling a prototype that was double tracked. The other reason is for modelers whose leanings are strongly on the railfan side

who want a more casual "let 'em run" scenario, where a train can just cruise on one main line while they switch and operate on the other.

Moving from a single main line to a double-track format introduces some design considerations:

• Parallel track separation must be adequate, especially on curves

• Double-track layouts require slightly more space to accommodate the extra line

• Crossover locations require significant length and their locations

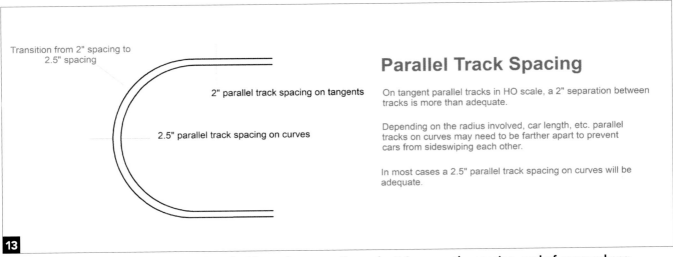

Parallel Track Spacing

Transition from 2" spacing to 2.5" spacing

2" parallel track spacing on tangents

2.5" parallel track spacing on curves

On tangent parallel tracks in HO scale, a 2" separation between tracks is more than adequate.

Depending on the radius involved, car length, etc. parallel tracks on curves may need to be farther apart to prevent cars from sideswiping each other.

In most cases a 2.5" parallel track spacing on curves will be adequate.

13

Parallel track spacing becomes crucial on double-track curves. If you don't increase the spacing, end-of-car overhang (especially with passenger cars and 60-foot and longer freight cars) may cause cars to sideswipe.

14

The double-track main line at right has back-to-back crossovers, protected by interlocking signals. This is on the CSX main in Rockville, Md. The double-track Metro line at left separates to go around the commuter shelter.

15 Crossovers eat up a lot of linear space on model railroads. The two HO scale Atlas no. 6 turnouts of this crossover stretch to roughly 18".

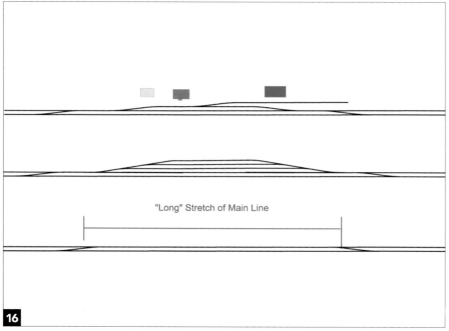

"Long" Stretch of Main Line

16 Plan for crossovers before and after each town or industrial area (top), before and after yards (middle), and periodically along long stretches of main line (bottom). "Long" is subjective, but you probably don't want to have more than 15 or 20 feet of main line without a crossover.

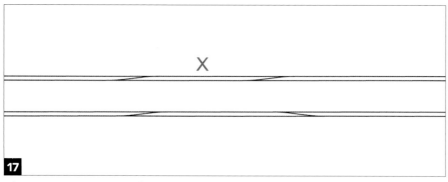

X

17 Alternate crossovers so they create a series of sidings (bottom). Avoid the top orientation.

need to be carefully planned

• As with the prototype, double-track layouts entail more expense and time to build (due to extra track and turnouts) as well as more maintenance

Separation between parallel tracks must be sufficient to keep trains from sideswiping when meeting. For parallel track on straights I use a 2" track spacing in HO, 1" in N, and 3.6" in O. Curves are a different matter because the ends of cars overhang outside the curve. The overhang on the train on the inside curve can contact trains on the outside track.

The amount of increased separation needed on curves depends on the track geometry, curve radius, and length of rolling stock, **13**. As a general rule, 2½" in HO and 1¼" in N will keep you out of trouble. Also, the risk of collision is greater the deeper into the curve you are, so you can transition into the separation. Don't rely on math alone: Test your curves with equipment you'll be using, then test it again after installation but before adding ballast so you can make any needed adjustments.

The need for adequate track separation means double-track layouts require more space. This becomes an issue more with layout room width than length. Take a typical around-the-walls shelf with center peninsula design: You'll need an extra 2" on each side shelf plus 2" more on each side of the peninsula for a total of an additional 8" of layout width.

Double-track main lines require the need to cross from one track to another, **14**. Planning the location of the crossovers (back-to-back turnouts connecting the lines) is important because you need to access key areas such as yards and industrial spurs from each main track. You'll also need crossovers for passing.

This is a key issue because crossovers take up *lots* of linear space: A crossover in HO with no. 6 turnouts is roughly 18" long, **15**. For a crossover near a curve you'll also need to add 4" to 6" more as a buffer between the turnout and curve. Crossovers *on* curves should be avoided—they require complex, expensive trackwork and introduce reliability issues. This all means crossovers will reduce the amount of space you have for other elements (such as industrial spurs).

When designing a double-track layout, do a thorough mental operational run-through when locating crossovers to ensure that trains have adequate access to yards, towns, or industrial areas on the other track. You'll need a crossover before the element is reached and another on the other side to get back, **16**.

Watch the orientation of each crossover so it acts as a siding so trains can cross from one track to the other and then back without a backup move, **17**. Place crossovers *before* a yard throat, not midway through the yard. You'll also want the ability to occasionally switch from one track to the other mid-run, especially on larger layouts.

Regarding turnout sizes: Larger is always better, but we have to face the reality of limited space. In most cases I use no. 6 turnouts and have done so without operational problems. When a train passes through a crossover and then must immediately traverse another turnout or curve—entering a yard, for example—there is a lot of back-and-forth whipsawing going on. A straight-track buffer between curve and turnout will improve reliability, **18**. You can also sometimes adjust the placement of the crossover, **19**.

Not all crossovers will be in space-starved locations on a layout. Where they're on a long run of expansive scenery, I'll often increase the turnout size to no. 8 or even no. 10 for better appearance.

Keep in mind that a double-track layout requires significantly more track than its single-track counterpart. There's a material cost associated with the second line, plus the required crossovers. Along with the cost of the crossover turnouts themselves comes hidden costs such as switch machines, stationary decoders, and control panel switches and other wiring. In addition to the financial cost is the additional construction time and increased maintenance.

Some of my clients request a combination of double- and single-

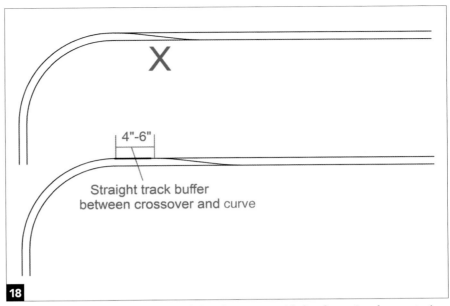

In order to minimize the chance of derailments, avoid the dynamic where a train exits a curve and then immediately runs through a crossover (top). Allow a 4"-6" transition buffer of straight track between the curve and crossover turnouts as shown in the lower arrangement.

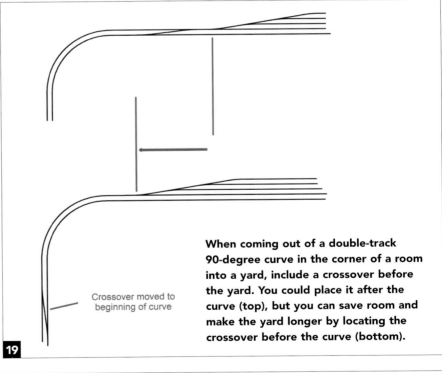

When coming out of a double-track 90-degree curve in the corner of a room into a yard, include a crossover before the yard. You could place it after the curve (top), but you can save room and make the yard longer by locating the crossover before the curve (bottom).

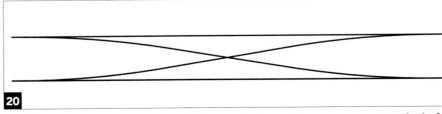

Double crossovers are rare on prototype main lines, but can save a great deal of space on a layout.

If you have long stretches of double track in rural areas, you don't need to always keep the two lines parallel. You can add visual interest by separating the lines in spots, as here on the Burlington Northern in northwest Illinois. *Jeff Wilson*

track main lines. While such an approach works visually (which may be enough) it subtly but substantially creates a major change operationally. As soon as you have so much as a foot of single track on a double-track layout, you've effectively created a single-track layout with very long sidings. With a pure double-track layout you truly can just let two trains cruise—one on each of the mains. The instant you single-track just a portion of the line, you'll need to pay close attention to avoid a collision on the single-track portion.

A double crossover is a double-track arrangement with two pairs of turnouts and a crossing in the middle, allowing trains on either track to pass to the other main, **20**. They save linear space, as they take the same footprint as a standard crossover, but they are complex. They are more common as space-savers on model railroads than on prototype railroads, which avoid crossings whenever possible. Prototype railroads opt for back-to-back standard crossovers whenever space allows.

Another consideration of double track is that, especially in rural areas, the two main tracks sometimes aren't parallel. They can split to traverse geographical features such as hills and waterways, **21**. This can be done to provide a more-favorable grade on one route or to better cross a river or other obstruction; it's also sometimes done when a second main is added after the first and there's not enough space to build a parallel track along the original. In any case, it can add visual interest to a scene.

Transitions and easements

A vital aspect of layout design from a mechanical reliability standpoint relates to transitions from curves to neighboring elements such as turnouts, lift-out bridges, and S-curves, **22**. When layout construction starts, modelers often devote a lot of attention to dimensional accuracy in placing track in the "exact" spot it appears on the drawing. Realistically, that degree of precision isn't usually necessary.

However, what *does* matter is how smoothly we transition from one element to another. If the transition is too abrupt, say from curve to turnout, derailments are the end result. What we want to avoid is the mechanical "whipsaw" dynamic of trains moving too quickly from curves to turnouts and from too-abrupt reverse (S) curves, **23**. The solution generally involves putting a straight section between reverse curves as a buffer. This requires space, but the improved reliability makes it worth it. Broad-radius S curves, **24**, look good and operate more smoothly, but can still benefit from a buffer tangent.

The same concept applies to turnouts at entrances of sidings which, when you examine them closely, are essentially S-curves. This is the reason I recommend against sharp (no. 4) turnouts, as the transitions in the turnout geometry are too harsh, **25**.

There are two ways to enter a curve. One is to simply go from straight track directly into the set curve radius, **26**. The other is to make a more gradual transition via a spiral of decreasing radius: an "easement." Without question, easements look great aesthetically, and they have become popular in track-plan design over the past decade or two. I've found, though, that our trains are moving slowly enough that easements aren't really needed to improve mechanical reliability. My opinion is to use them if you find the look visually appealing, but don't worry about omitting them.

Classification yards

Many modelers immediately plan to include one or more visible yards in their designs because they are critical areas on prototype railroads (and centers of much activity), **27**. This, however, highlights a common mistake of layout design, which is to jump to the technical aspect of a design element before asking whether the element should even be included in the first place. Classification yards are a

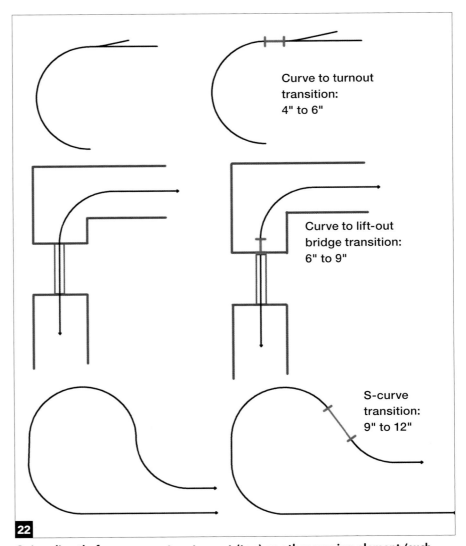

22

Going directly from a curve to a turnout (top) or other moving element (such as lift-out bridge, middle) can cause operational problems. One way to avoid potential issues is to insert a linear (straight-track) buffer between elements. Do the same with S-curves (bottom), avoiding situations where track curving one direction makes an abrupt turn in the other direction.

Curve to turnout transition: 4" to 6"

Curve to lift-out bridge transition: 6" to 9"

S-curve transition: 9" to 12"

major case in point.

Because yards take up an enormous amount of space and represent a lot of complex, expensive trackwork, thought should be given to what you're trying to accomplish with a yard before placing one or more indiscriminately within your design. A key to remember is that prototype yards are *not* designed to store cars—they're designed to sort cars and get them on their way again as efficiently and quickly as possible, **28**. Many great model railroads don't include visible yards. If yard operations aren't your thing, you'll probably be better served by using the space for another town, more industries, other

features, or to extend your main line.

Before adding a classification yard to your plan, ask yourself:
- Does the yard accomplish an operational purpose—specifically, to disassemble trains, re-classify cars, and then build new outbound trains? Do you care about this aspect of operations? Do you enjoy yard switching?
- Does the yard serve a relevant scenic purpose? In other words: Is the yard a signature scenic element on your prototype? A yard may be relevant to include visually even if you don't care about operating it.
- Are you a rolling-stock enthusiast

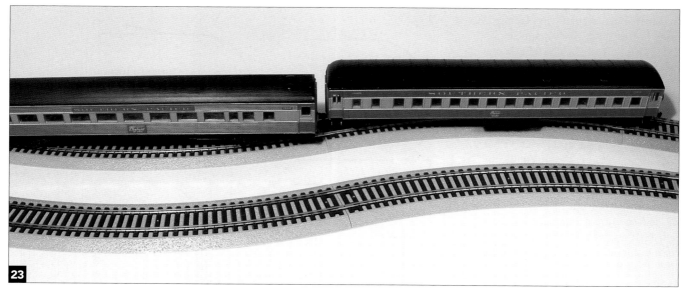

23

Sharp S-curves (24" and under in HO) create a "whipsaw" effect, where ends of cars (especially long ones) turn in opposite directions and resist alignment. Use broader curves or add straight track between curves. *Jeff Wilson*

24

Gentle S-curves are aesthetically pleasing and operate well, but note that there's a stretch of tangent track between the curves on this Conrail line at Red Rock, Pa. *J.J. Young Jr.*

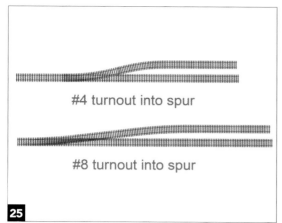

25

The S-curve effect applies to turnouts as well. This shows the sharpness of a no. 4 turnout at a siding entrance (top) compared to a much-smoother no. 8 turnout (bottom).

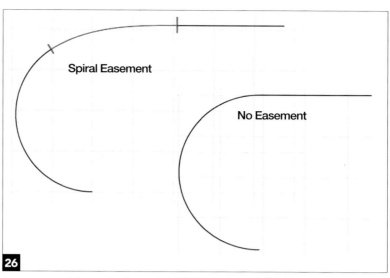

Spiral Easement

No Easement

26

An easement is a spiral transition into a curve (left). They look great but aren't mandatory to improve mechanical reliability. You can go directly from straight to curve as shown on the right and be fine.

27 The New York New Jersey Rail yard in Brooklyn is a reasonably small, modelable facility. It illustrates the true function of a yard, specifically to break down and classify cars. It's *not* to store and showcase rolling stock. Note the generally uncongested look and the number of open tracks.

28

Several switchers are simultaneously working Burlington's yard in St. Paul, Minn., in the 1940s. Railroads keep cars moving in yards. *Chicago, Burlington & Quincy*

29

If you think storage will be the primary purpose of a modeled yard, consider instead eliminating the yard and adding open storage shelves next to the layout as an alternative.

looking at a yard as a display platform? If so, I'll point out that with the exception of the front track or two, you're going to be looking mostly at the tops of cars. A display case will accomplish your purpose more effectively.

• Do you look at a yard as a storage facility? If so, I'd encourage you not to add one for that purpose. Doing so will clog up the tracks, making it difficult to carry out its true function. A separate storage shelf is better, **29**.

• If your primary satisfaction comes from just watching trains run through scenery, railfan-style, you may be able to get by with one small yard, or if you just run a few trains, no yard at all. Ditto if your interest is way-freight and mainline train operations.

Let's look at the features of a typical prototype yard. At first glance, a yard looks like just a big collection of tracks. However, each track has a specific purpose, and in designing a model yard, we should likewise make sure each track has a reason for being there, **30**. Prototype yards vary widely in size, **31**, and in a perfect world it would be great to include all of these features, but in the real world we are so short on space we often don't have that luxury. The number of features you include will largely be driven by the amount of space you have available. You can accomplish a lot operationally in a small yard of just three or four tracks.

Key yard elements to consider are:

• **Arrival and departure tracks.** Arrival tracks are where incoming trains are spotted. Once there,

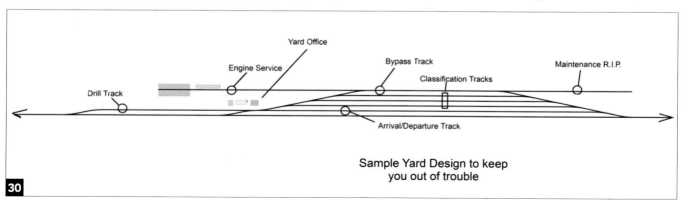

Yard Office

Engine Service

Bypass Track

Classification Tracks

Maintenance R.I.P.

Drill Track

Arrival/Departure Track

Sample Yard Design to keep
you out of trouble

30

Each track in a yard has a specific purpose, regardless of yard size. Some prototype yards have just two classification tracks; others have dozens. Your available space will dictate what you include on your design.

the locomotives and caboose are removed and a switcher begins pulling cars to the classification tracks. Departure tracks are where outgoing trains are constructed, and where locomotives and a caboose are added. If space permits and you have a lot of traffic, separate tracks are nice; if space is at a premium, a single track or two can serve both purposes.

- **Classification tracks.** The yard switcher sorts cars on separate tracks based on final destinations. For example, track 1 is for destination A, track 2 is for destination B, etc. Once the classification is done then the blocks are moved to the departure track to build the train.
- **Drill track.** The drill track is a long lead extending from the classification tracks. It allows a yard switcher to push and pull long strings of cars from the classification tracks without fouling the main line or other tracks. If space permits, it should be as long as your longest yard track. More on these in a bit.
- **Engine servicing.** This is where locomotives are fueled, serviced, and stored until called into service. Depending upon location and era, these can range from a small diesel refueling pad on a single track to a massive roundhouse and shop area.
- **Storage tracks.** Yards are designed to keep trains moving, but they still have tracks for storage. This included

31

The Minneapolis & St. Louis yard at Peoria, Ill., circa 1946, is a small, modelable design. The engine house is the quanset building at left. *Henry J. McCord*

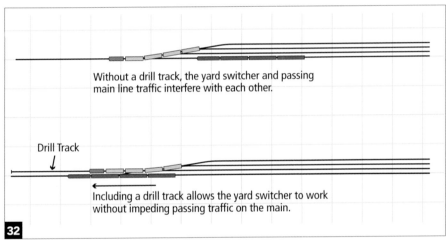

Without a drill track, the yard switcher and passing main line traffic interfere with each other.

Drill Track

Including a drill track allows the yard switcher to work without impeding passing traffic on the main.

32

A drill track is a key element in a model railroad yard, because it allows the yard switcher to work without fouling the main line.

33

John Colombo models the Nickel Plate Road in 1957 in N scale. His model of the Bellevue, Ohio, yard is 16 feet long on a 28"-wide shelf. The engine facility, with 18-stall roundhouse, is in the distance at left. *John Colombo*

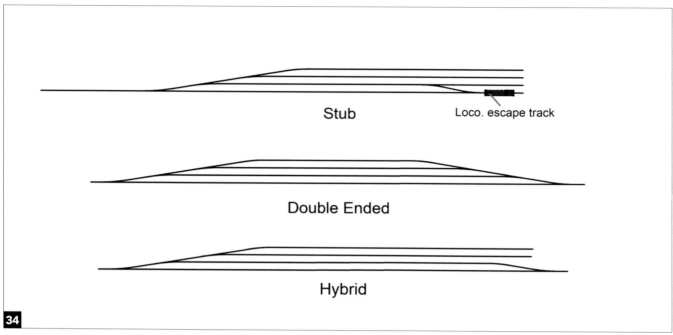

Stub

Loco. escape track

Double Ended

Hybrid

34

Yards can be stub ended, double ended, or a combination of the two.

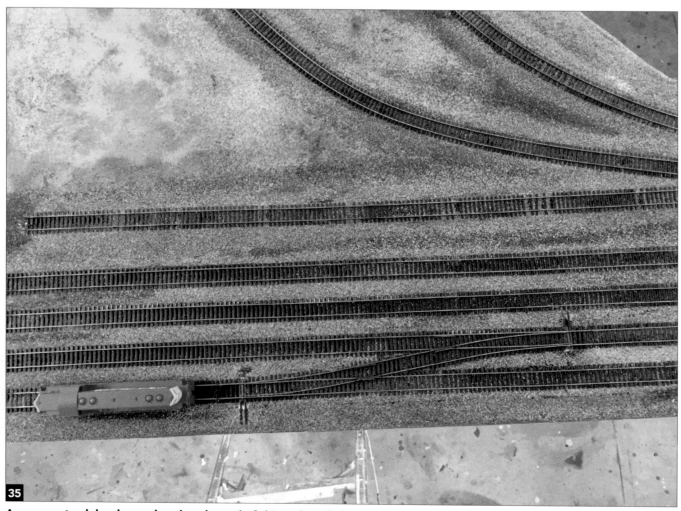

35

An escape track has been placed at the end of this stub-ended yard, allowing the engine to get out from behind its train on the arrival track.

36

The stub-end staging yard for this layout is at the end of the peninsula at left.

37

This stub-ended staging yard on Tony Koester's old HO Allegheny Midland was hidden from the layout, but was easily accessible in an adjoining room. *Tony Koester*

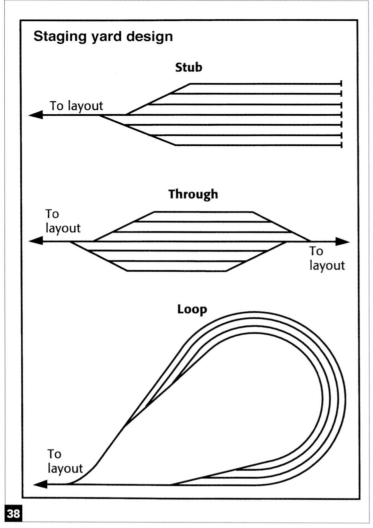

Staging yard design

Stub

To layout

Through

To layout

To layout

Loop

To layout

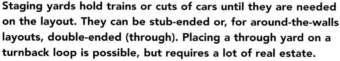

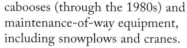

38

Staging yards hold trains or cuts of cars until they are needed on the layout. They can be stub-ended or, for around-the-walls layouts, double-ended (through). Placing a through yard on a turnback loop is possible, but requires a lot of real estate.

39

cabooses (through the 1980s) and maintenance-of-way equipment, including snowplows and cranes.

• **Repair tracks.** Minor repairs to rolling stock are performed at a track and small shop area known as the RIP (repair-in-place) track (which might be more than one track). Some larger yards had extensive facilities for major car repairs or rebuilding.

In designing a yard, give primary thought to keeping the activities of yard switchers separated from passing trains on the main line. If your layout plans include running through trains along with switching a yard, you'll quickly find you run into a problem—

specifically, a traffic jam as a train approaches the yard and confronts a switcher on the main pulling a cut of cars. You don't want the poor yard crew to constantly stop working and wait for the main to clear.

The solution is the drill track, **32**. A drill track is nothing more than a long lead parallel to the main that allows the switcher to work without fouling the main line. Although available space won't always allow it, ideally the drill track should be as long as the longest yard track. Working a drill track into the yard design goes a long way toward streamlining future operations.

Yards take up an enormous amount of room, **33**, because of the length

of the turnout ladders (consecutive turnouts leading to parallel tracks). And remember, as the previous chapter highlighted, turnouts almost always take more space than an initial pencil-sketch design allows—you'll find this especially true when designing yards.

Yard designs fall into three basic categories: stub-ended (the ladder on only one end), double-ended (also called "through," with a ladder on each end), or hybrid, with a mix of stub-ended and through tracks, **34**. Stub-ended designs save a lot of space because you eliminate one ladder while allowing longer tracks; however, since they can only be worked from one end, they are very cumbersome and limiting

There's no reason you can't scenic a visible staging yard, as Ken Karlewicz did on his HO scale Delaware & Hudson Second Subdivision layout. *Ken Karlewicz*

from an operational standpoint. Inbound trains can end up with the locomotives trapped at the end; an escape track (crossover) will allow them to escape, **35**.

Double-ended yards are easier to operate, but need to be significantly longer to allow the same length of tracks as a shorter stub yard. Operationally, you are better off going with a double-ended or hybrid configuration; available space will ultimately make the decision for you. For a more in-depth look at yard design, I highly recommend Andy Sperandeo's book, *The Model Railroader's Guide to Freight Yards* (Kalmbach).

Staging yards

Layouts—even large ones—represent a relatively small geographic region that hypothetically connects to a much larger outside world. A primary goal of layout design, visually and operationally, is to create the illusion that this is the case. Staging tracks and staging yards allow us to do this, **36**.

A staging yard is essentially a holding zone "behind the theatrical curtain" that represents the rest of the world beyond the visible layout. Trains wait in staging until it's their turn to enter the show, proceed onto the layout, and then either return to that same yard or another one on the end of their run. The illusion is that the

trains are coming from distant cities, arriving on your layout from, say, a neighboring division—not a hidden track in an adjacent room.

Pioneers of layout design such as Tony Koester have written extensively on the subject, and popular model railroads from the 1970s and onward (notably Tony's Allegheny Midland, **37**, and Nickel Plate Road layouts, Allen McClelland's Virginian & Ohio, and Bill Darnaby's Maumee Route) follow these design principles.

Before getting into staging yard design, determine first if you actually need one. If you model a line that will only have one train—an out-and-back branch or city industrial line, for

40 Santa Fe modeler David Barrow, a proponent of open staging, built this double-ended open staging yard on his HO Cat Mountain & Santa Fe Ry. The near end represents the east end of the line as East Hill. The other end is called West Mesa to represent the western end of the railroad. *Tommy Holt*

Staging through a wall into another room (or through a backdrop divider) can be disguised by a bridge, tunnel, structures, or other features. This is the exit to staging on David Gallaway's HO layout. *David Gallaway*

example—you may not (or perhaps just a staging track or two). If you're more of a railfan with limited interest in prototypical operations, you *may* not, but you might find staging helpful if you plan to run a variety of trains.

The actual configuration of staging will largely be driven by the size and shape of your available space. A key planning consideration is how many tracks to include. For example, your east-end staging yard will not only need enough tracks to hold your outgoing westbound trains, but also enough empty tracks to accept incoming eastbound trains.

You have two basic formats available to you, **38**. The ideal design is a continuous run loop layout design with one double-ended staging yard serving both directions, a concept written about and championed by

David Barrow. This allows trains to seamlessly come and go in both directions, and inbound trains will automatically be restaged—in position and pointing in the proper direction for the next operating session.

If your layout is a point-to-point format, then the likely solution is a stub-ended staging yard on each end of the route. These serve the operational purpose well during a session, but require a lot more work to re-stage trains between sessions (including handling locomotives by hand to move and re-orient them). A variation of this is a return loop yard at each end, but few modelers have the tremendous amount of space required, especially to make multiple return tracks long enough on a loop with a switching ladder at each end.

In determining how many staging

tracks you need—in many cases with space restrictions—the more accurate question is "how many can I squeeze in?" Ideally, take the number of trains heading in one direction (eastbound for example) and double it.

With that said: Having operated on many layouts, one thing I commonly witness is—in a perfectly understandable effort to display a layout in all its glory—a tendency to run too many trains, have too many operating crews, and not allow enough time between trains. The end result is a three-ring circus that stresses operators and strains staging capacity.

Being more realistic about a layout's operational capacity and having fewer trains, but focusing on their operations (for example, perhaps simulating 8 or 12 hours of a day instead of 24) usually results in less-hectic, more-enjoyable

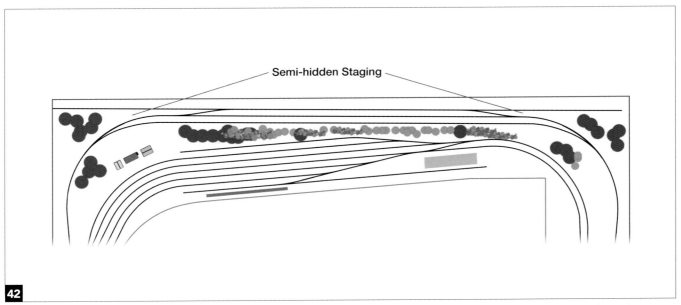

42

One possible staging compromise is to position the staging tracks or yard toward the back of the layout shelf, but keep the top open and the tracks within easy reach. Downplay the yard by slightly screening it off visually with a row of low-lying trees or structures.

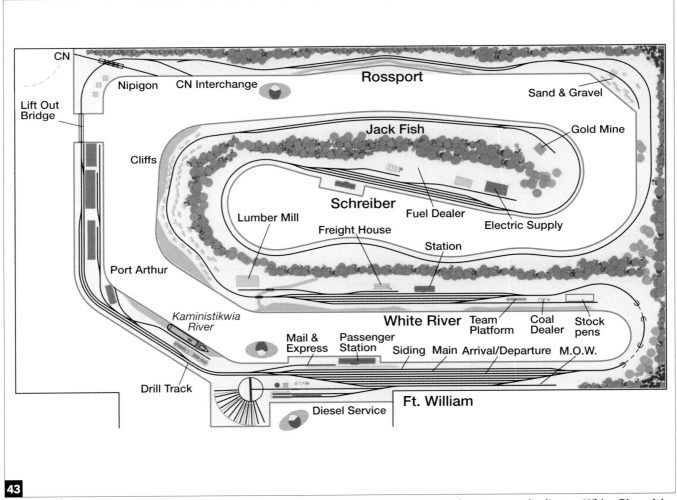

43

Modeled yards can also serve as staging. In this plan, trains start at Fort William and run across the line to White River. It's essentially a case of labeling and frame of mind, but Fort William and White River "could" be thought of as staging.

44 This diesel servicing area on the Peoria & Pekin Union at Peoria, Ill., is simple, with a sanding tower and fuel tank (converted tank car) in the middle, with locomotives from several railroads on adjoining tracks. *J. David Ingles*

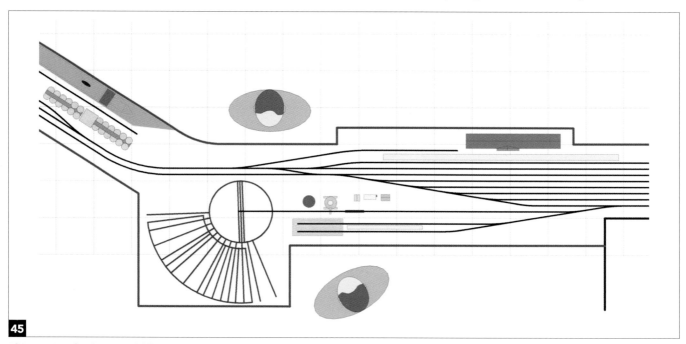

45 This engine facility would be appropriate from the steam through early diesel eras. The room design made it possible to locate the roundhouse where it was easily accessible. Not all room shapes allow this luxury; roundhouses often have to be truncated, with fewer radial tracks and stalls. Turntables became far less common by the 1970s.

sessions that also allow reducing needed staging capacity.

Staging yards can either be in plain view (open staging), **39, 40,** or away from view (hidden staging), **37.** Open staging yards can be scenicked like other areas of the layout, and offer the benefits of easy access to the trains and track. A downside is that it hinders the illusion that trains going to staging are leaving to go to (or coming from) another place far away.

Hidden staging carries the illusion better, with yards blocked from view of the layout and the entry track disguised by a bridge, **41,** tunnel entrance, or trees. The challenge of hidden staging is potential limited access to the track. It's ideal if you have room to place hidden staging on shelves easily in reach—as through a doorway and around a corner.

Hidden staging can become problematical when tracks and yards are tucked in separate rooms (without direct adjacent access) or in tight, restricted spaces—such as behind a water heater or furnace. These hidden yards may seem like a great solution on paper, but once built (or even *while* building it), owners often quickly realize what a nightmare they can be. Cars can be hard to see; reaching in to couple, remove, or re-rail cars is arduous. Cleaning track can be difficult or impossible. Derailments will occur in the worst possible spots. If you can't avoid hidden staging, proceed with your eyes wide open, knowing that you're making a significant design choice.

A compromise is semi-hidden staging, with tracks behind a line of trees, structure flats, hill or ridge, or other low-level view block, **42.** Another compromise is having a visible classification yards at one or both ends of the main line that can also serve as visible staging yards, **43.**

Locomotive servicing

How you approach the design of a locomotive servicing facility will be driven by a number of factors unique to your situation. Do you model the steam era? Steam-to-diesel transition? Early diesel? Modern? Are you looking at a light-duty diesel refueling facility, **44,** or a classic full-blown steam servicing area with turntable and roundhouse, **45?**

As with yards, you should start by asking yourself the basic question of whether you actually need an engine facility. Do you want one just to show

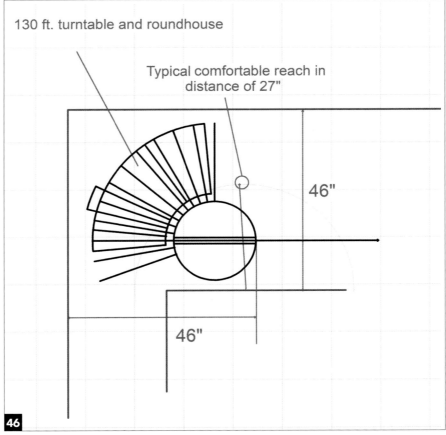

46

Multi-stall roundhouses encompass a huge footprint and in many cases put you in a situation where locomotives on the service tracks are beyond reach (something to avoid if at all possible!).

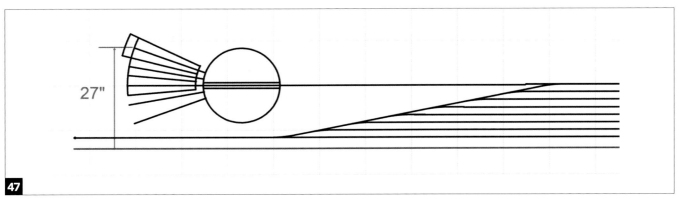

47

Having fewer radial tracks shrinks the footprint considerably, making reach-in distances more manageable.

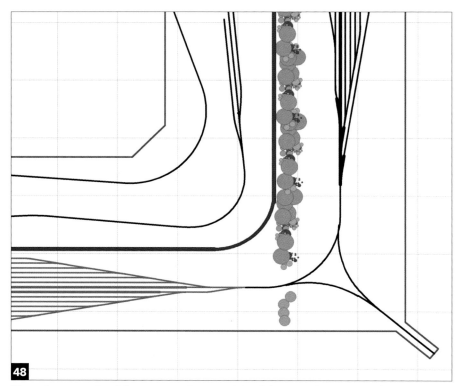

48

If you have ample aisle space and use an island format, the corner of the layout can work for a wye.

off your locomotive collection, or will it be a key part of your operations? Are you following a specific prototype facility that is a signature item for your model railroad, or can you adapt elements based on your available space?

By and large, servicing facilities tend to dovetail nicely and fit seamlessly into the triangular empty space at the top of a yard ladder, with one exception: the roundhouse. Some modelers consider roundhouses a vital structure, but be aware that as the number of stalls increases beyond three or four, they begin to take up an enormous amount of room, **46**. Because of their size, radial nature, and turntable length, planning for reach-in distances becomes a major consideration. If you include one, make every effort to locate the roundhouse in a position (preferably near the layout front), where reach-in access is best. The fewer stalls and radial tracks, the easier your life will be, **47**.

Consider the era when designing your facility. Roundhouses were disappearing fast by the 1960s, and turntables became much less common by the 1970s.

Wyes are an alternative to turntables, and are used by many prototype railroads to turn locomotives and other equipment. Operationally they are easier to install and less-expensive than turntables, but they can present significant design issues on a model railroad. They are huge space eaters and can be very challenging to fit into many room spaces, **48**. One might not think this would be the case, but the need for broad enough curves between the turnouts and a wye stub track length long enough for a long locomotive (or a locomotive plus a car) means they're almost impossible to fit onto a shelf.

Best practices

In the next chapter we will start pulling everything together. Before we do so, let's address a house-cleaning matter: some "best" practice specifications to help keep you out of trouble and on the straight and narrow.

As you start designing a layout, it's nice to have a set of standard specifications for the technical parts of a design. I realize that my telling you "it depends" regarding several factors

likely won't be very helpful, but it's the truth. With that disclaimer, I'll go out on a limb with the following guidelines. Although in my experience there is no one-size-fits-all answer, there certainly *is* a one size fits most. In other words, these best practice standards aren't absolute, but most will keep you out of trouble. If you want to push the limits of some of them, you may be able to—but definitely be conscious of what you're doing, do some testing, and use these as a starting point.

Minimum turnout size: no. 6

Parallel tangent track spacing: HO: 2"; N: 1"; O: 3.6"

Parallel track separation at curve apex: HO: 2⅜"; N: 1¼"; O: 4½" (Be sure to test!)

Maximum grade: 1.75 percent

Minimum radius, 4-axle diesels (or medium steam), 60-foot cars: HO: 24"; N: 12"; O: 43"

Minimum radius, 6-axle diesels and 89-foot passenger/freight cars: HO: 34"; N: 17"; O: 60"

Track setback from fascia: 3" (farther if possible)

Track set in from backdrop: 4" (minimum)

Transition straight track between end of curve and turnout: HO: 4"-6"; N: 3"-4"; O: 6"-8"

Maximum reach-in distance to track: 27"

Layout height: Armpit level

Aisle width: One person alone: 24"; multiple operators: 36"; wider is always better

Comfort matters

It's a natural tendency to get caught up in an all-out effort to squeeze as many of your dream elements into a design as possible. In doing that, we tend to subconsciously make compromises and concessions in the areas of human comfort. During the excitement of initial construction you may not notice these compromises, but you eventually will. Too-narrow aisles, too-broad reach-in distance, and too much hidden track almost always leads to regret. If your layout is too uncomfortable to interact with, you'll enjoy it less and less, perhaps even to

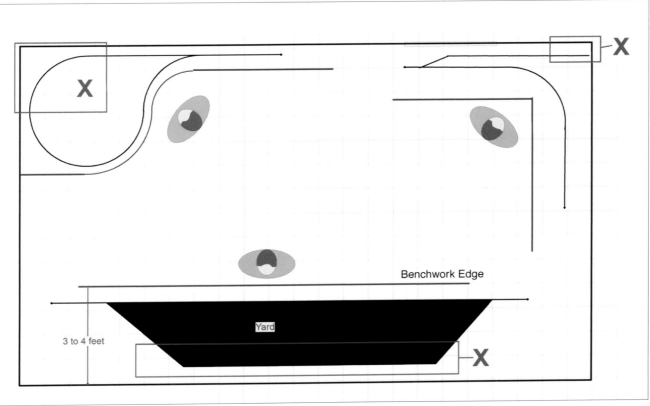

49

the point of not wanting to deal with it at all.

I want to emphasize minimizing reach-in distance. Consider it *vital* from a design standpoint that *all* track be close enough to the fascia so that you can easily reach it, **49**. The key word is "easily": Standing awkwardly on a stool, popping up like a prairie dog through removable access hatches, or hanging from a ceiling joist don't qualify as "easy." Don't delude yourself about this: You'll need to clean your track, you'll need to uncouple cars, you'll need to nudge stalled locomotives, and you'll need to fix derailments (and experienced modelers will agree on Murphy's Law of model railroading: If a train derails or an engine stalls, it will happen at the hardest-to-reach, most-inaccessible part of the layout!).

Comfortable reach-in distance varies depending on your height and the height of the benchwork. It's vital that you know *your* number, and the only way to do that is to test it on a mockup. Set a piece of track on a table or shelf the exact height of your layout, extend your arm, and note the distance

you can comfortably place a car on the track.

Be wary of all hidden track. We've already discussed hidden staging, but also beware of track in tunnels, in structures, or behind backdrops, tree lines, structures, or other view blocks. Rest assured that at some point you will need to access hidden track to fish out a car. Don't minimize the frustration of such "fishing trips." A good design limits—ideally to zero—the amount of hidden track. If you need to have track pass into a structure, make the roof removable or the entire structure removable so you can gain access if need be.

The one exception I make to jumping through hoops in order to squeeze more elements into a design is the lift-out bridge. I think their advantages far outweigh the inconvenience and construction. Unless you have steps coming into the center of the plan, in order to make an around-the-walls shelf design work you

will need to be able to enter the inside area of the layout and the lift-out is the only way to do it.

In *all* cases I recommend a lift-out as opposed to a duckunder. My reasoning is that you can always leave a lift-out section in place and duck under it, but not vice versa. Keep in mind that the older we get, the less easily we can simply duck under a layout (an important consideration if you have older operators on your crew). Also, you'll have periods where you spend more time building than operating, and it's a simple matter to just remove the lift-out, set it to the side, and walk easily into and out of the layout.

Layout height and aisle width
When it comes to your layout feeling comfortable, getting the layout height correct is high on the list. There is no one specific height (and you'll see much debate on forums and in the hobby press), but I've found in general

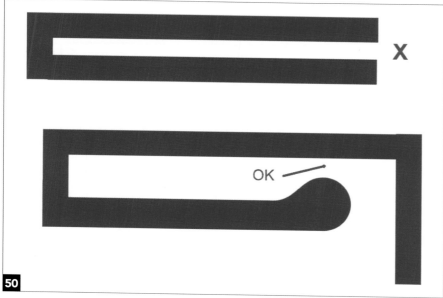

50

Long, narrow aisles (top) should be avoided. However, pinch points (short sections of narrow aisle) can be workable as long as the aisle opens wider on each side (bottom).

The 3 functions of track on a model railroad

There are three possible purposes any given section of track can serve on a model railroad. When pulling your design together, if a section of track doesn't serve any of them, you must ask yourself: "Why am I including it?" The three purposes are:

1. Operational necessity. This one is obvious: For example, as a minimum you need one track to get from Town A to Town B.

2. Operational interest. For those who enjoy operating a layout prototypically (or believe they will in the future), tracks that serve industries, allow trains to pass, and allow sorting cars (yards) are worth including. For operators who employ timetables and train orders and enjoy hours of carefully sorting cars at a complex industrial park, yard, or town a yard, it makes sense to add track that supports this aspect of the hobby. However, if you're a railfan-type hobbyist for whom this isn't your idea of fun, and if you just enjoy watching trains roll through scenery, it makes no sense to add tracks for something that doesn't interest you.

3. Scenic interest. For those trying to re-create a pleasant memory centered around a specific rail scene past or present, including all of the track in that scene is key to capturing the feeling and emotion of the memory. These modelers want to copy that scene and be transported there. Copying the trackwork elements that are a part of that scene makes sense, even if it means adding track you may not use operationally. The track itself essentially becomes three-dimensional art.

Note that prototype railroads only care about the first item on the list: operational necessity. They don't want track that is "interesting to operate" and they don't spend millions on track because it looks interesting. A railroad's objective is to use as little track as possible to move cars from point A to point B efficiently and profitably. Keep this in mind as you design your track plan.

terms a track level that is at about armpit level is the most comfortable and provides the best viewing experience. It is such an important consideration that I suggest mocking up a shelf at your planned height, putting a piece of track and a train on it, and seeing how things look and feel. Also, if you model in a smaller scale such as N, you may want to bump the height up slightly higher to make viewing easier.

It's relatively common for a client to tell me they want a layout low so their grandkids can see it. Keep in mind that kids grow, and quickly (perhaps more quickly than your construction speed!). Don't design for a child's current height—design for *your* height and let the kids grow into it.

Aisle width plays a crucial role in terms of how comfortable a layout is to interact with. A critical factor is how many people will be operating on the layout and how often you'll have guests. In my experience, 95 percent of the time it's just the layout owner running solo. If that's your case you can go narrower. If you expect frequent guests, you'll need to go wider.

Again, prepare a mockup. Pull a kitchen table close to a wall, put boxes on top to get the height up to what the layout will be, and see firsthand how different aisle widths feel. Move your table closer and farther from the wall to see how it feels. Another factor is aisle length. Longer aisles should be wider. Aisles don't need to be the same width everywhere. You can have "pinch points" where things are narrower if it opens up on each side, **50**. If you have a larger, serpentine layout, it's a good idea to have some places inside where things open up a little.

My personal layout has aisles that are 30" to 33" wide, and that feels comfortable to me, even with three or four guest operators. I have one narrow pinch point at 20" (a planned compromise), but it's not that comfortable. Also, avoid busy features on opposite sides of an aisle, **51**—these quickly result in human traffic jams.

Another design pitfall to avoid if possible is getting cut off from your train. Operators want to be able to

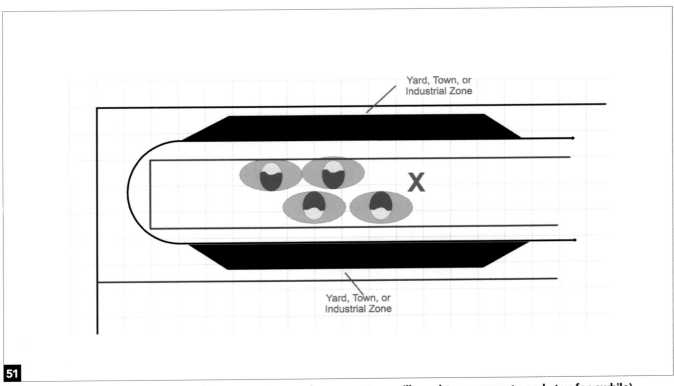

51

Avoid putting two high-activity switching zones (areas where operators will need to congregate and stay for awhile) directly across the aisle from one another.

walk along shelf benchwork and down the aisles and follow their trains as they traverse the layout. Avoid design situations where you get cut off from your train and need to walk long distances to catch up to it. This can happen with peninsulas, **52**.

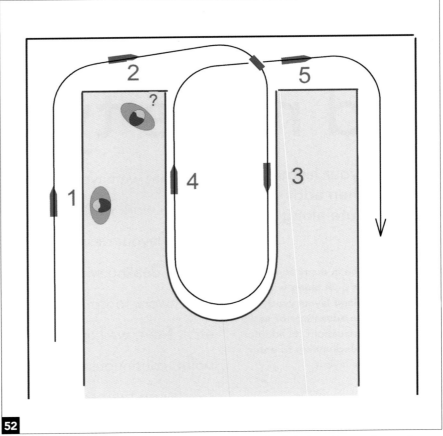

52

In this design, operators are cut off from the path of their trains as they enter the peninsula. Avoid this situation if possible.

1

CHAPTER FIVE

Benchwork footprints and route types

Designing your layout "canvas," then adding a mainline route along it

Benchwork can be in many styles, including shelves built along walls or free-standing. Island layouts such as this one have the advantage of easily clearing wall obstructions. In addition, you don't need duckunders to enter the center of the layout.

Now that we have an understanding of the basic tools we have to work with, we can combine them to develop an overall layout design, **1**. In creating a design, conceptually we are dealing with two primary elements. First we have the benchwork footprint style (shelf, shelf with peninsula, island, etc.). Next, we have the track plan's mainline route (point to point, continuous run, or return loop), which we will draw/ overlay on the benchwork.

Here's the plan of attack we'll be taking to develop the layout design. As we go through each step, you'll be putting various elements in place where they fit in the overall context.

1. Choose your benchwork footprint style

2. Select your route type

3. Overlay the route type on the benchwork footprint

4. Take the section of the prototype you want to model and convert it to a schematic

5. Overlay that schematic on your route

6. Add secondary track and details

This chapter will focus on the first two steps: the benchwork footprint and route type. Working with the two entails a bit of the "chicken or the egg"—you need to have at least a rough conceptual understanding of both as you come up with an overall concept. There will also likely be some back and forth as you explore various combinations. The benchwork is the "canvas," onto which you will "paint" the track plan. We'll start with the benchwork, as that is driven by your room shape and is less flexible in terms of options.

Benchwork footprints

Let's begin with a reality check. The space we have is the space we have. No amount of wishing, squinting, or hand-wringing is going to make that 20x20 basement grow to 20x30. Accepting that reality—accepting and embracing our constraints—is the first step toward a great design. Take a step back and examine the room you have available from a neutral, dispassionate viewpoint and take a deep breath: No matter what your situation, something immensely rewarding can be placed in that space.

Analyze your space: How do you enter the room, **2**? Is the door at a corner? In the middle of a wall? Is there a staircase into the center (if so, you're extremely lucky)? What are the wall obstructions (windows, doors, electrical boxes)? Are there other objects in the way (furnace, water heater, sump pump, other utilities)? Will closets need to remain in service

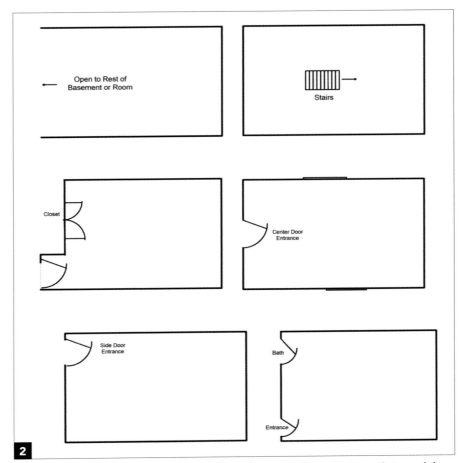

2

Here are some of the more-common room shapes and layout areas that model railroaders face. We can design layouts to fit all of them.

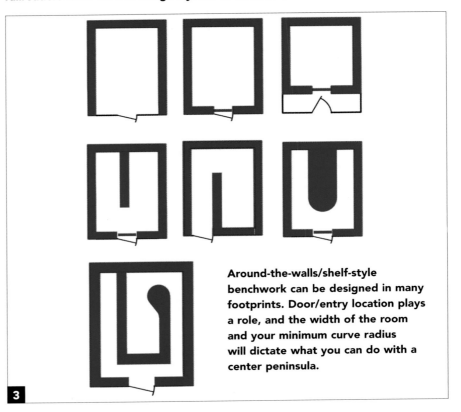

3

Around-the-walls/shelf-style benchwork can be designed in many footprints. Door/entry location plays a role, and the width of the room and your minimum curve radius will dictate what you can do with a center peninsula.

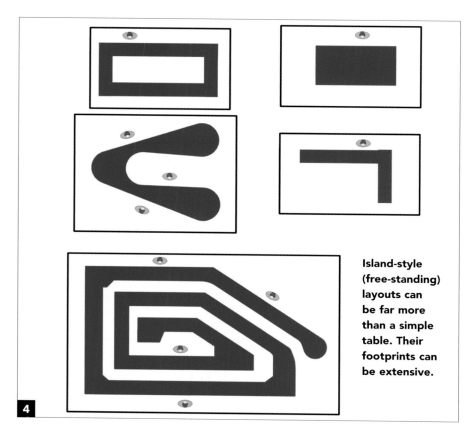

Island-style (free-standing) layouts can be far more than a simple table. Their footprints can be extensive.

4

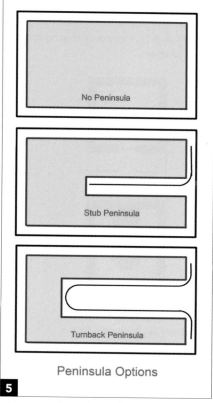

No Peninsula

Stub Peninsula

Turnback Peninsula

Peninsula Options

5

There are three basic formats for an around-the-walls shelf design: with no peninsula, a stub-end peninsula, or peninsula with turn-back loop.

At the most basic level you are going to choose one of two benchwork footprint styles. Either you will line the walls with shelves in a way that clears obstacles in the room, or you will place a free-standing island in the middle of the room.

Shelf layouts have increased in popularity in the past few decades, **3**. They offer a number of advantages: they generally provide the longest run length for most spaces; they allow broader curves; and shelves can be narrow and simple in construction. Operators can easily follow their trains. Potential disadvantages include the necessity of a duckunder or lift-out section in many cases, and having to clear obstacles around the walls and in the room.

Free-standing islands have largely fallen out of favor in recent times, but they can be a viable option, **4**. They usually make it easy to follow trains, with no need for duckunders and no issues with windows, doors, or wall obstacles. Downsides include a generally shorter mainline run, tighter curves, more complex benchwork, and difficulty in adding staging yards.

Free-standing layouts can work well in larger spaces. Keep in mind that in smaller rooms, table or island-style layouts actually take up more space than the layout itself. For example, with a "standard" 4x8-foot layout—although a popular option for many beginners—if you add a minimal 2-foot aisle around all sides, it actually requires an 8x12-foot footprint.

For the most part, if you have a typical 20x20-foot basement space or anything smaller with minimal obstructions and want to maximize your mainline run, the shelf style will almost always be your better option. If you have a larger space and want to eliminate the need for duckunders, the island format deserves a hard look.

Shelf-style benchwork

If you choose some form of shelf style benchwork, you then have three basic variations to pick from, **5**: around-the-walls with no center peninsulas; around-the-walls with a stub-type peninsula; or around-the-walls with

or can the doors be removed? What is the overall room size? Visualize where aisles might be placed.

Why go through this exercise? Historically, most modelers have a pre-ordained track plan in mind (often from a magazine or book) and, come hell or high water, they are determined to find a way to squeeze, contort, hammer, pound, and shoehorn that idea into their space whether it lends itself to it or not. The result? A plan that doesn't work as intended, with comfort compromises, mechanical/reliability issues, and aesthetic compromises.

However, if you take the opposite approach, looking with an open mind at your available space as a clean slate onto which you can design a plan especially for it, you will have a much greater chance for success. The key is to *first* select a benchwork format that is workable for your space and go from there. This also plans for the future: I've known modelers who have left benchwork from previous layouts in place, scraped the old layout off, and built an entirely new layout on top of the old benchwork. It's an efficient, intelligent, pragmatic approach.

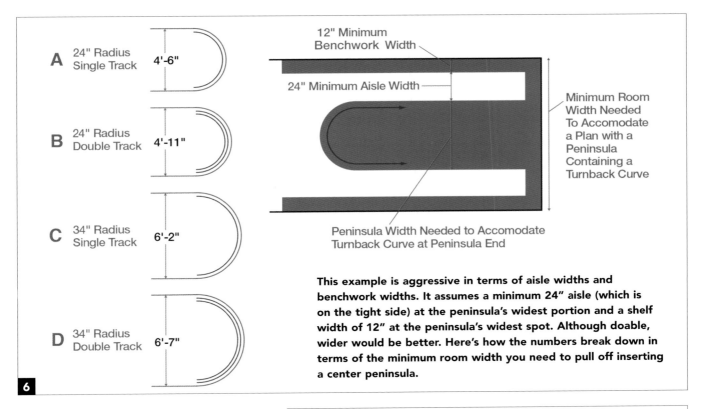

A 24" Radius Single Track — 4'-6"

B 24" Radius Double Track — 4'-11"

C 34" Radius Single Track — 6'-2"

D 34" Radius Double Track — 6'-7"

12" Minimum Benchwork Width

24" Minimum Aisle Width

Minimum Room Width Needed To Accomodate a Plan with a Peninsula Containing a Turnback Curve

Peninsula Width Needed to Accomodate Turnback Curve at Peninsula End

This example is aggressive in terms of aisle widths and benchwork widths. It assumes a minimum 24" aisle (which is on the tight side) at the peninsula's widest portion and a shelf width of 12" at the peninsula's widest spot. Although doable, wider would be better. Here's how the numbers break down in terms of the minimum room width you need to pull off inserting a center peninsula.

6

a peninsula wide enough to contain a turn-back curve at the end (this option is only viable if you have a wide-enough room for it).

Shelf formats with no peninsulas are straightforward enough and easily fit into any room shape. However, peninsulas with a 180-degree turn-back loop take up a *lot* of space and will only be viable if the room is wide enough, so adding one needs to be planned carefully. Let's follow the steps of checking to see if you have enough space for this option, **6**.

The space such a peninsula occupies is driven by your minimum radius and whether you are dealing with single or double track, **7**. Remember that for double track, the outside track will be 2½" outside of the inner minimum-radius track (for HO). You'll also need to allow a minimum of 3" between

Center peninsulas take up an enormous amount of space. Use them sparingly (only one per layout). Remember that the width of the peninsula is more than the diameter of the curve: You'll need at least a 3" buffer between the rail and fascia (preferably more depending on your scenery treatment).

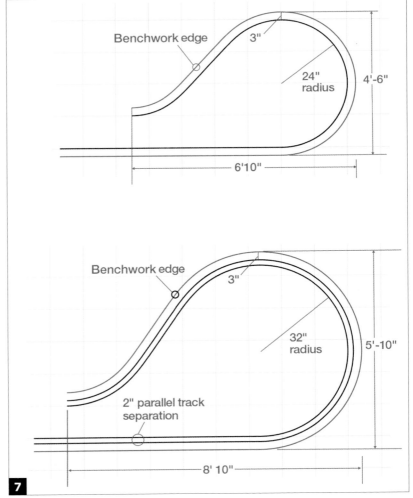

Benchwork edge

3"

24" radius

4'-6"

6'10"

Benchwork edge

3"

32" radius

5'-10"

2" parallel track separation

8' 10"

7

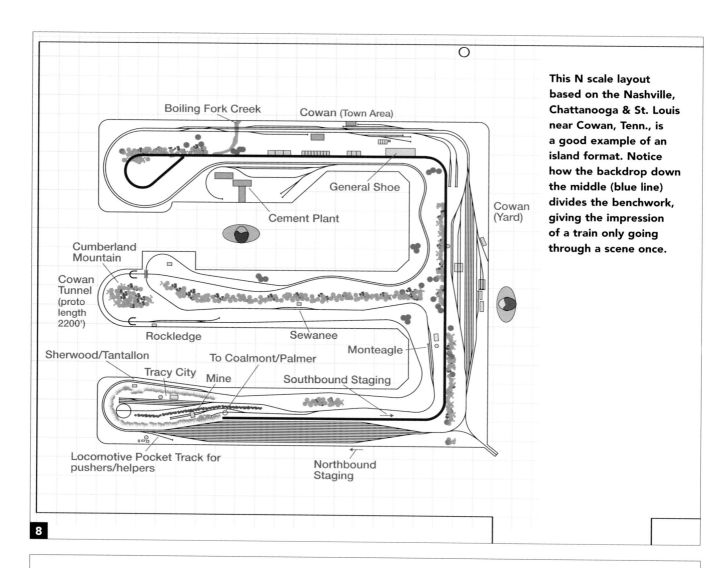

Boiling Fork Creek

Cowan (Town Area)

General Shoe

Cement Plant

Cumberland Mountain

Cowan Tunnel (proto length 2200')

Cowan (Yard)

Rockledge

Sewanee

Monteagle

Sherwood/Tantallon

Tracy City

Mine

To Coalmont/Palmer

Southbound Staging

Locomotive Pocket Track for pushers/helpers

Northbound Staging

This N scale layout based on the Nashville, Chattanooga & St. Louis near Cowan, Tenn., is a good example of an island format. Notice how the backdrop down the middle (blue line) divides the benchwork, giving the impression of a train only going through a scene once.

8

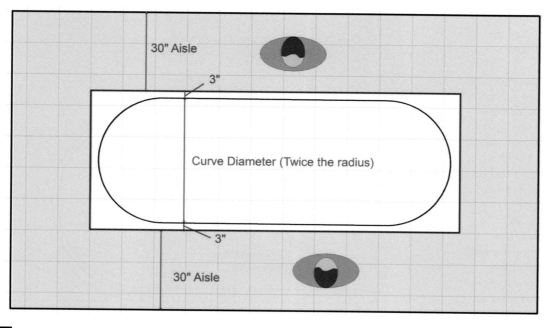

30" Aisle

3"

Curve Diameter (Twice the radius)

3"

30" Aisle

Here's how to calculate whether you have enough room for an island-style format. This assumes, in HO, four-axle diesels and 50-foot and shorter cars, allowing for a 24" minimum radius.

9

10 Tom Johnson only needed a benchwork depth of 12" to execute the above scene on his HO layout. *Tom Johnson*

the outermost track and the fascia (regardless of scale). For this exercise let's assume a minimum 2-foot aisle is needed on each side of the peninsula and a minimum of 12" of benchwork depth on the surrounding walls.

- 24" radius, single track: Room width needed: 10'-6"
- 24" radius, double track: Room width needed: 10'-11"
- 34" radius, single track: Room width needed: 12'-2"
- 34" radius, double track: Room width needed: 12'-7"

If, after running these calculations, you discover you have the available room width, then a peninsula with a turn-back loop is at least a viable option. Whether you choose to go that route is a different decision. Also remember that these are minimums: Do you plan to have a town, industries, or other track on the end of the turn-back peninsula? If you want any straight track on the end, you'll need to allow even more space.

Island benchwork footprint

For many model railroaders, duck-unders and lift-out bridges are deal breakers. The free-standing or island format solves that problem. If your

room has numerous doors, windows, and wall obstructions, the island may make more sense than a shelf format. Running a dividing backdrop or viewblock down the island center gives the illusion of increased size and hides the fact that it's an island, allowing two viewing perspectives for any given run of benchwork.

An island doesn't need to be rectangular or donut-shaped. It can be any free-flowing form that sits in the middle of the room—like, well, an island—and doesn't touch the walls, **8**. Some very large layouts have been built using this format. If you have the room, this can be a very viable format that is extremely comfortable to interact with. On occasion I'll get a client that has the luxury of a fairly large outbuilding dedicated for a layout, and in almost all of these cases we opt for an island format.

Determining whether an island will fit a room comfortably can be challenging. Islands are less flexible than shelf designs, so we need to do some math to see if one will fit, **9**. Again, the radius of your curves will be a driving factor. There are three components in play: aisle width, the curve diameter you will be using, and

an allowance between the track and fascia. As a best practice starting point start with a minimum aisle width of 30". Could you go tighter? Possibly, especially if you will be running solo. As with shelves, allow at least 3" between the outermost track and the fascia.

Let's do the math for a layout with 24" minimum radius curves:
- Allowance for aisles: 2 x 30" = 60"
- Offset between track and fascia: 2 x 3" = 6"
- Curve diameter: 2 x radius (24") = 48"
- Room width needed: 114" (9'-6").

Keep in mind that this is the *minimum*. If you want broader curves or some straight track on the end of that island, the room will have to be wider.

Benchwork depth

An ongoing theme of this book is that of letting the benchwork footprint drive the design (as opposed to drawing the track and contorting the benchwork to follow). The space you have is the space you have, and for most spaces there will only be a handful of viable benchwork alternatives. Previously we discussed

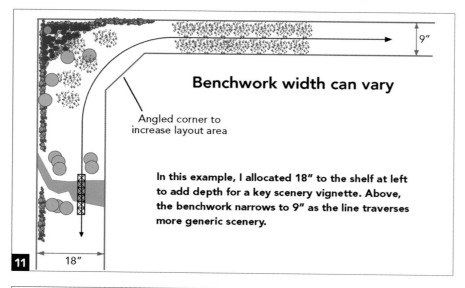

Benchwork width can vary

9″

Angled corner to increase layout area

In this example, I allocated 18″ to the shelf at left to add depth for a key scenery vignette. Above, the benchwork narrows to 9″ as the line traverses more generic scenery.

18″

11

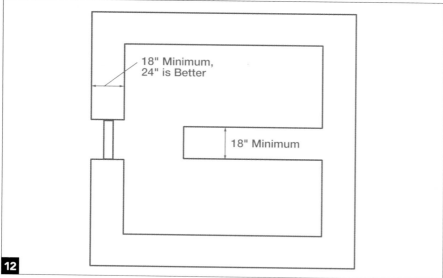

18″ Minimum, 24″ is Better

18″ Minimum

12

This quick sketch shows minimums for structural stability for freestanding layouts or components. Benchwork that protrudes into the room and is too narrow will tend to wobble and can suffer damage if bumped. Examples include peninsulas and benchwork on each side of a lift-out bridge.

the configurations themselves; now let's take a quick look at the subject of benchwork widths.

What is the ideal width? The short answer is the minimum width that carries out your scenic objectives and is also structurally sound (free of wobble), **10**. The narrower the benchwork, the more room for aisles, the simpler the construction, and the faster you'll be able to scenic the surface area. As a rough rule of thumb I start most designs with a width of 18″ to 24″ and then adjust from there. On my own layouts I've had a habit of making the benchwork much wider than I really needed to "get the message across." This increased construction time and reduced aisle width.

If your primary goal is operation, and your objective in a specific area is simply to create a sense of distance between points A and B as the train traverses Midwestern scenery, then you can go very narrow—as little as 8″ as noted modelers Tony Koester and Bill Darnaby have shown us. If the goal is a scenic vista or city/town with some depth to it, you can go wider, but keep in mind that maximum reach for most people is 27″. That means that even with a stool to stand on while you "plant trees," anything over 36″ in depth is difficult to work with. It doesn't have to be the same on each wall—it can vary to adapt to other features, **11**.

Finally, structural stability factors in. If you have a peninsula protruding into the room or a lift-out bridge dividing

13

Lift-out bridges are often necessary to enter the center of a layout. The simpler you can make the design, the better.

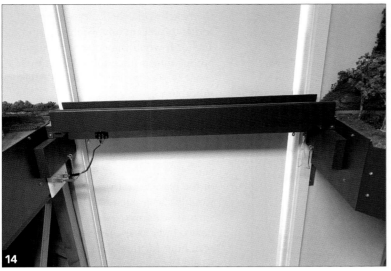

14 A bridge supported from the bottom is cleaner looking and doesn't extend into the layout scenery. Pins at each end keep it aligned.
David Galloway

15 A top-supported bridge is easier to build and tends to automatically stay aligned, but it doesn't look as clean.

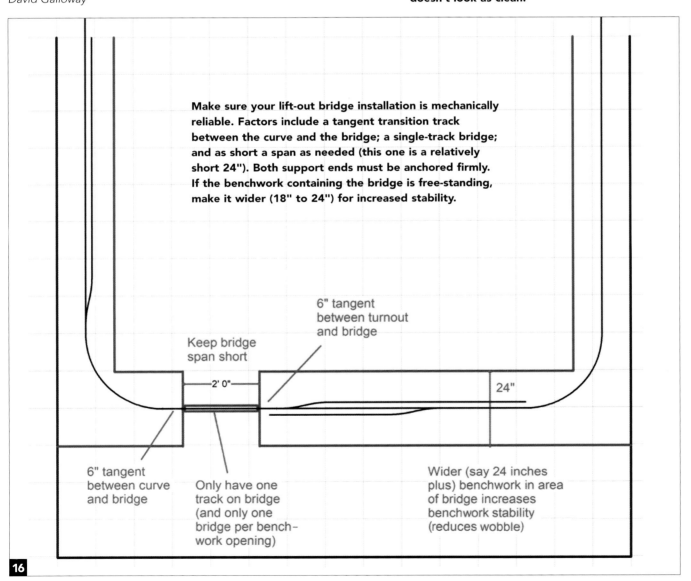

Make sure your lift-out bridge installation is mechanically reliable. Factors include a tangent transition track between the curve and the bridge; a single-track bridge; and as short a span as needed (this one is a relatively short 24"). Both support ends must be anchored firmly. If the benchwork containing the bridge is free-standing, make it wider (18" to 24") for increased stability.

Keep bridge span short

6" tangent between turnout and bridge

—2' 0"—

24"

6" tangent between curve and bridge

Only have one track on bridge (and only one bridge per bench-work opening)

Wider (say 24 inches plus) benchwork in area of bridge increases benchwork stability (reduces wobble)

16

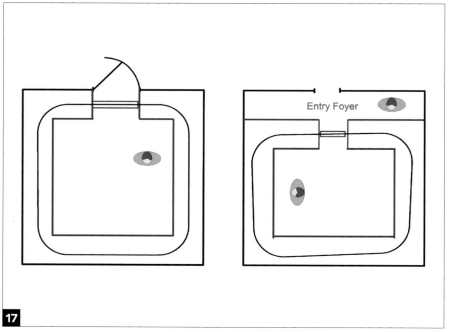

17

If your room has a centrally located entry door, you can build the layout tight against the wall, providing a mid-benchwork lift-out and the longest run length. Another option, which works for any door position, is to set the benchwork back 30" or so against the wall, creating an entry foyer.

the benchwork, you'll need more width to prevent any wobbling (and to anchor it when someone accidentally bumps into it forcefully), **12**. In these areas 24" is suggested, with 18" the minimum.

Entering the layout

In a perfect world, we'd be blessed with a room configuration where a staircase conveniently delivers us into the center of the basement. In addition, walls wouldn't have such rude intrusions such as windows, doors, electrical boxes, and closets. Like many, I've been searching for this place called "a perfect world," but realize that it rarely occurs. That leaves us with a situation where, with a shelf format and continuous-run design, we need a way to get to the center of the layout.

That leaves two variations of the same option: the lift-out, **13**, or duckunder. The duckunder always looks like an easy solution on paper, but all

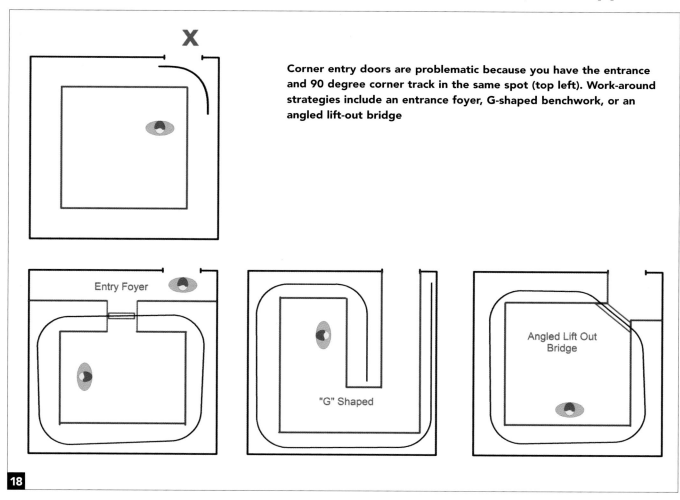

Corner entry doors are problematic because you have the entrance and 90 degree corner track in the same spot (top left). Work-around strategies include an entrance foyer, G-shaped benchwork, or an angled lift-out bridge

18

19

Double-deck benchwork, as here on Tony Koester's HO Nickel Plate Road layout, introduces many challenges and complexities. It can be a viable option for modelers wanting the longest possible main line for operation. *Judy Koester*

too often leaves the builder years of asking "What was I thinking?" as aging knees and hips need to droop to stoop under the layout—and a guaranteed knot on the head on occasion as you stand up too quickly. And you don't realize how many times you do this, for both construction and operation, until you actually have a duckunder.

That leaves as the preferred option to be the lift-out (bridge) section. Remember: You can always leave a lift-out in place, making it function as a duckunder, but you can't do the reverse and turn a duckunder into a lift-out. Although not ideal, I've found that a lift-out bridge is the one compromise to ergonomics that is generally worth it terms of opening up better design options. Also, layout owners generally spend more time building than operating, so when you aren't running trains the bridge can be simply set aside and allow easy access.

Modelers have used a number of designs for lift-outs, **14**, **15**, and some have built swinging gates as well. Articles on their construction have been published in magazine articles and books. Here are a few things to keep in mind regarding lift-out design and construction, **16**:

- **Keep it simple:** I can't emphasize this enough: The simplest design is generally the best. As soon as you begin planning devices such as swings, pulleys, and elevators, you're opening a can of worms. Every unnecessary complexity opens up new possibilities for misalignment and mechanical trouble. A basic plank is the best. Supporting the bridge from the top, as opposed to the bottom, ensures alignment.
- **Make it single track:** The fewer tracks crossing the bridge, the simpler your life will become. One track is best. Wood expands and contracts; benchwork moves. You'll have to make periodic adjustments, and you don't want to deal with adjustments to several tracks every time you set the bridge in place.
- **Give it a wide, stable base:** Keeping the benchwork wider in the bridge area makes it more stable. Make the bridge wide enough that a derailed car won't go over the edge (or add railings to the sides of the bridge).
- **Make track straight, not curved:** Try to have at least 6" of straight track on each end of the bridge and its approach tracks.
- **Shorter is better:** Keep the bridge span short: 24" is good; 30" if needed for a doorway.
- **Limit lift-outs:** Limit the number of lift-outs per opening to one and preferably only one per layout.

The location of the entryway into the layout room impacts the design alternatives and often in a big way. The smaller the room, the larger the impact. In an ideal situation, the door is in the middle of a long wall, and the lift-out

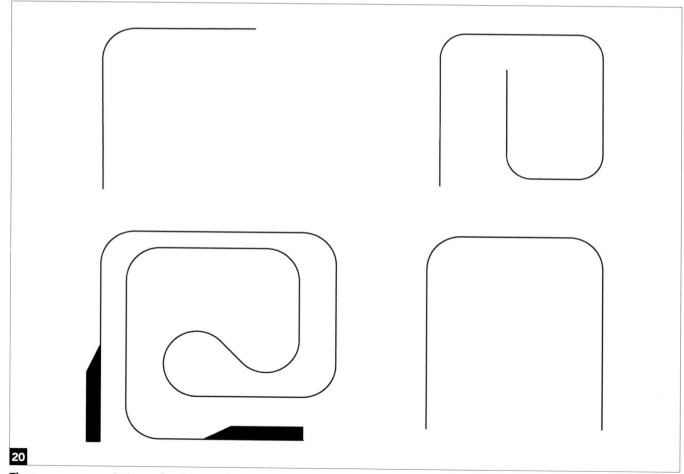

20

There are many variations of point-to-point route schematics; they can be twisted into many different shapes.

can be directly at the door. We need 90-degree curves at each corner of the layout. If the entrance door of, say, a spare bedroom is at the corner of the room, this becomes difficult because it squeezes out the 90 degree bend.

One way of dealing with this is adding an entry foyer, **17**. This allows you to move the lift-out anywhere along the front edge of the layout where it works best; the disadvantage is losing a few feet of layout, as the design essentially shortens the side walls. Other options are shown in **18**.

Double-deck designs

"I'd like a long mainline run. I'll just build a double- (or triple-) deck layout." Modelers often say this as if it's as simple as snapping two pieces of sectional track together. I hear it frequently from excited modelers new to the hobby. There are some nice ones out there, **19**, but multi-deck layouts introduce far more complexities than a single-deck layout of the same square footage. Building them isn't simple or easy, and unless you have significant layout construction experience, I don't recommend them.

Multi-deck designs have their place and, for the experienced modeler, they do solve the goal of a much longer run length. However, it comes at a significant cost in materials, expense, and construction time. Don't even consider a multi-decker unless you are fully aware of the complexity and compromises they entail. With respect to a double-deck layout, ask yourself, "Does the value of 'what's up there' (meaning what's on the other deck) grossly exceed the agony, cost, and compromise associated with getting there?"

With multi-deck benchwork, there are two basic designs: two levels connected by a helix, or a lower-level shelf that gradually increases in elevation around the walls until it climbs atop itself, with stub-ended yards on each end.

Double-deck layouts have basically one "pro" (but a big one for timetable-and-train-order operation fans)—a longer mainline run. If operations are your main interest and you feel this is

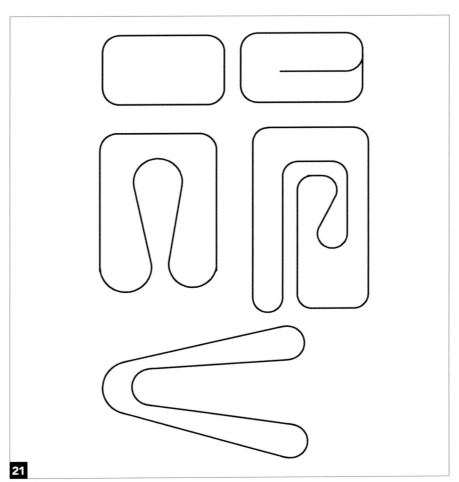

21

Here are some common continuous-run schematics.

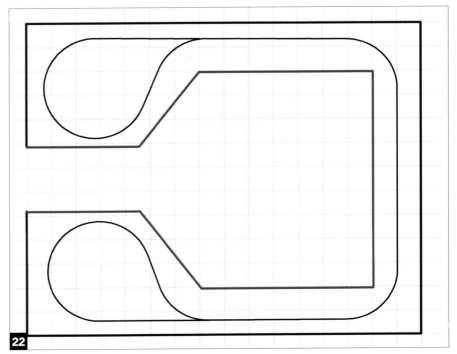

22

The "dog-bone" return-loop design was a popular format in earlier decades. Because of its drawbacks (lots of space required for loops; the rear track of each loop is beyond reach-in distance) it's no longer as common.

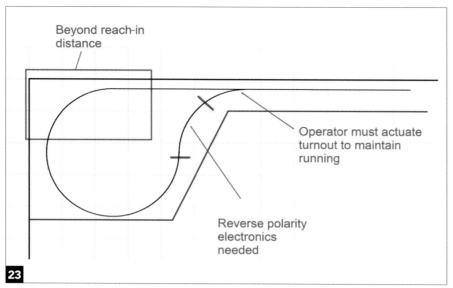

23

Return loops can be useful to turn trains, but they also present a number of drawbacks, particularly if they're located in the corner of a room.

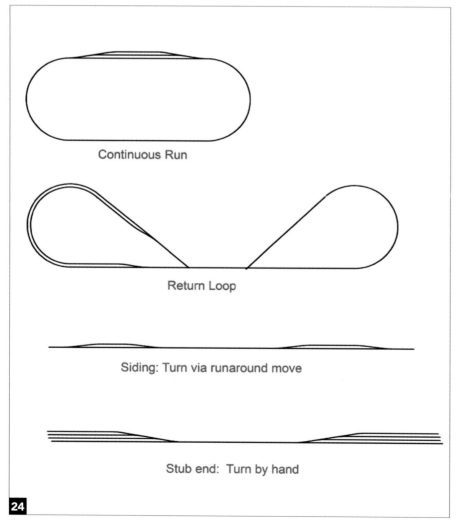

24

With a continuous-run or return-loop plan, turning (or "re-staging") a train is basically automatic (top two diagrams). With a point-to-point plan you'll often need to handle some of the re-staging manually (bottom two diagrams).

worth it, go for it. Be aware that multi-deckers have many challenges—here's a quick list:

• Complexity of building a helix (grade; access limitations; percentage of mainline run within the helix), plus the large footprint size of a helix

• Neither deck will be at the ideal height

• Vertical clearance on lower deck limits height of taller structures such as grain elevators; upper deck presents challenges in below-track-level features such as valleys and rivers

• Lower-deck lighting can be challenging, especially under wide upper decks (separate lights are often required)

• The need to avoid having one high-activity area directly above another on the lower deck

• Overall benchwork complexity and layout size

Space precludes going into great detail on the many aspects of these layouts here. If you are pondering a multi-deck layout, check out Tony Koester's *Designing and Building Multi-Deck Model Railroads* (Kalmbach) for details on design, benchwork, and construction.

Route types: The track plan schematic

Now that we've established the shape of the layout foundation—the benchwork footprint—we can move on to the next step: deciding in general terms the format of the mainline route we want to overlay on top of it. At the most basic level there are two configurations: point-to-point and continuous run. However, if you view the route schematic as a piece of string or rubber band, these options can be curved, stretched, and formed into almost limitless shapes and configurations, **20, 21**.

A hybrid configuration is a point-to-point design but with a return loop at one or both ends, **22**. Return loops were common in track plans into the 1970s, but have largely fallen out of favor in the past few decades. Although there are situations where

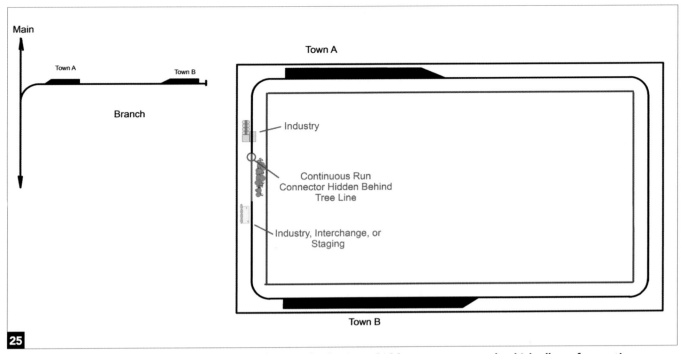

25

Even if your prototype is an out and back branch, consider having a hidden connector track which allows for continuous running when possible. Your room shape will dictate whether this is viable or not, but it's a feature worth considering. During operating sessions, the connector can be disguised as an industry lead.

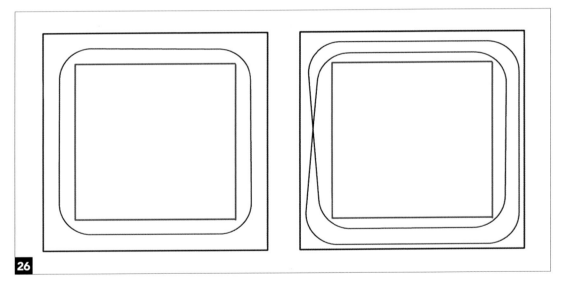

26

The diagram on the left is a "pure" design—a train only passes through each scene once, which is what you'd see in the real world. In the diagram at right, with a folded loop, a train passes through each scene twice. This isn't realistic, but it does double your run length.

return loops have merit, the drawbacks tend to outweigh the benefits, **23**. While continuous-run designs allow a train to cycle the layout with no interaction, return loops don't allow that luxury: You'll need to flip the turnout at the beginning of the loop as the train passes the other direction. That defeats the purpose of allowing trains to cycle unattended.

Return loops also require special wiring to deal with the change of electrical polarity. They take up a tremendous amount of space for what you get in return operationally (and keep in mind that the loop track must be longer than your longest train). If the loop is pushed into a corner, as is often the case, reach-in distances become a serious problem. For these reasons, I generally try to avoid using them in my designs.

Continuous run vs. point to point

One of the most important design decisions you need to decide early on is whether you want a continuous-run or point-to-point plan, **24**. There is no right or wrong decision, just what's "right" for you. The key is to have a crystal-clear understanding of the pros and cons of each so you can make an informed decision that you'll ultimately be happy with.

Although there are no absolutes, those who are more of a casual railfan and in the let 'em run camp usually lean toward continuous run. The point-to-point format is more popular within the pure prototype or operations crowd, particularly if they're modeling the ever-popular branchline scenario.

A number of considerations factor in, including your preferred running style, whether you're a prototype modeler (and the specific prototype and stretch of railroad you're modeling), and what your room size and shape will allow. One thing that's rarely talked about—but should be factored into your decision making—is the percentage of time you plan to spend running trains as opposed to building things. If your primary source of satisfaction is building as opposed to operating (and it is for many), the need for continuous running becomes less important.

Let's compare some of the differences. The most obvious is the ability to simply let trains run that

continuous run gives you. There's no denying the appeal of just letting a train or two cruise continuously around the layout with zero need for interaction on your part. Obviously with a point-to-point plan you have to stop the train at some point and either run the locomotives around the train to head the other direction, turn the locomotives manually, or bring another train out of stub-end staging.

Keep grades in mind. With a continuous-run plan, what goes up, must come down. If you climb an uphill grade you will be limited in that the run length needed to reach a specific summit height will need to be equaled to return back to your original elevation. You'll need to return to elevation zero to close the loop vertically, which will limit how high you climb.

With a point-to-point plan you can

climb higher vertically because there's no need to return back to elevation zero—an important factor if you're modeling a prototype on a mountain grade, for example.

With either design, as you plan for grades remember that towns and yards must be level, which limits the amount of run length you have available to close that loop vertically on a continuous run plan.

Finally, restaging trains is far easier with a continuous-run configuration. With a point-to-point plan, at the end of an operating session trains need to be restaged. Continuous-run plans lend themselves to double-ended staging yards where this isn't an issue.

Because you don't have to "close the loop," point-to-point designs are easier to work into difficult room shapes. Going a step further, they're just easier to design in general. Another

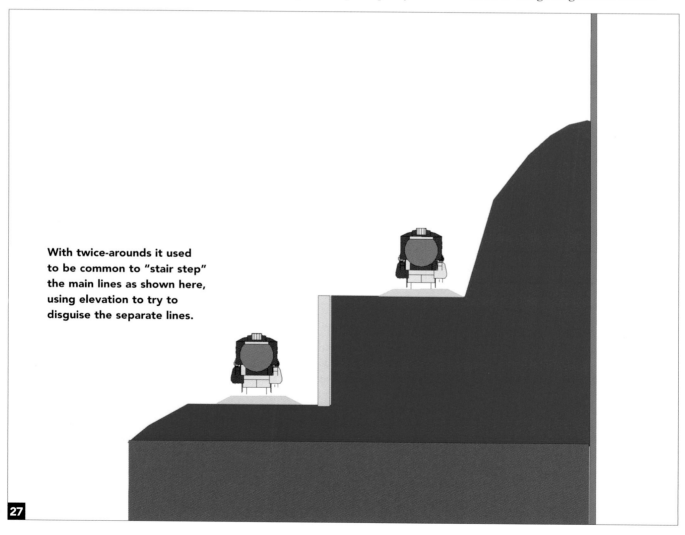

With twice-arounds it used to be common to "stair step" the main lines as shown here, using elevation to try to disguise the separate lines.

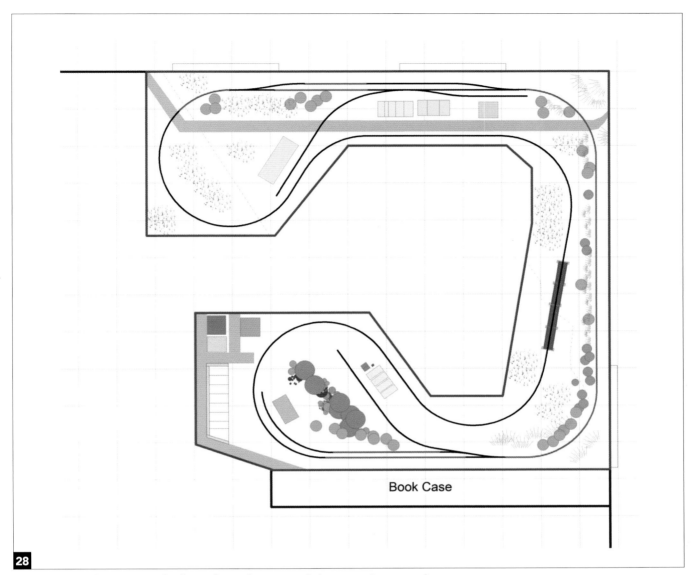

28

In this design the customer had very limited space and chose a twice-around to increase run length. Some scenery sleight-of-hand (track in red is hidden by trees) helps hide the fact that a train passes through each scene twice.

advantage of a point-to-point plan is that you don't need a lift-out bridge to enter the center of the layout.

You can make a continuous-run layout look like a point to point. Even in cases where you want a point-to-point design to capture the look of a branch line, it can nice to have continuous running capability if you can easily work it into the design (handy for cycling trains, breaking in locomotives, open houses, or times you just want to see trains run). There are ways to do this without it being obvious.

Enter the "continuous run connector." This is a portion of the loop that is screened off visually, hiding the fact that you do in fact have a loop, **25**. During an operating session, this connector can be ignored or—better yet—used as an industry track. When you want a continuous run you just cycle through the connector.

Defining a "pure" design

For most of us, the goal is to have a model railroad that is at least plausible if not highly realistic. To have a hotshot piggyback run by you in one direction and then moments later zoom by on a nearby track going in the opposite direction is a visually jarring deal-breaker from a design standpoint.

The phrase coined to address this situation is what is called a "pure design." In a pure design, there is only one scene in front of you between the fascia and backdrop, and the main line only passes through any given scene once. The emergence of pure designs became dominant by the 1980s, and were a vast improvement from many "blob" layout designs that were prevalent in the hobby's early days.

There may be situations where you have limited space but want more run length, so a twice-around main line may become a necessary evil, **26**. If you're forced into this, try to arrange the scenery and use trees, building flats, or other details to hide one of the two mains from view in each scene to downplay it, **27**, **28**.

1

CHAPTER SIX

Finalizing your footprint and route

Focusing on the benchwork and basic track plan

This is a free-standing layout, but it is basically an around-the-walls design with a small stub peninsula holding a staging yard. There's also a wye at the end where it joins the main layout.

We've spent a lot of time in previous chapters going through the benchwork footprints and route options we have available to us. It's now time to make the crucial decision as to how we want to combine the two, **1**. That decision will form the foundation of our design. The goal of this chapter is to finalize the benchwork footprint that works best for your space, finalize what route type you will use (continuous or point to point), and overlay the route schematic on top of that footprint.

Some important questions and decisions will emerge. The key is to know which factors come into play so that you can make an informed decision regarding which format provides the best tradeoff for your situation. First, you need to have the self-awareness to know whether you are a prototype modeler, operator, or casual/just-for-fun train runner.

In starting your design (and as you go through the process), give careful consideration to the following questions:

- How much layout do I want to bite off?
- Do I want continuous run or point to point?
- How important is total mainline length? If you are modeling one town it may not be important. If modeling multiple trains' journeys from town A to B to C, it becomes more important.
- Will the plan require a lift-out bridge or duckunder? If so, can you live with it?
- Does the track pass through a scene only once? If not, is the visual/operational tradeoff OK with you?
- Are you willing to have a return loop?
- Do you want a center peninsula? If so, do you have room for a 180-degree turn-back curve or will it be a stub?
- Are all reach-in distances manageable? Do any return loops create major access problems in a corner? Are there any other areas where track is more than 27" from the fascia?
- How many linear stretches does the design offer?
- If necessary, are there opportunities to add staging yards, including punch-throughs to adjacent rooms?
- Does the plan have a lot of hidden track? (This is easy to rationalize on paper but something you'll almost certainly regret later.)

Room example

Let's take a look at the common benchwork footprints available to us and compare their respective pros and cons using a typical room as an

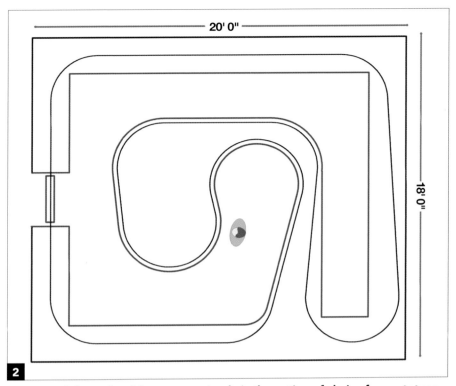

2

The around-the-walls with center peninsula is the option of choice for prototype modelers and prototype operators. If you need to take ergonomics into account (and you do) it is the most space-efficient design in terms of providing the maximum main line run per square foot. In most cases this is my preferred option when working with my customers.

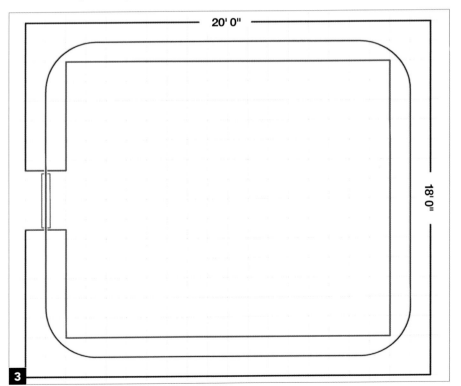

3

An around-the-walls, no-peninsula design is open and easy to build. It allows ample space for other features in the room. It's an excellent choice for a small branch or industrial line.

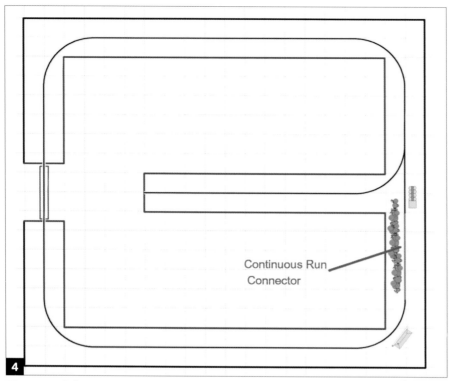

4

The around-the-walls with stub peninsula is versatile, allowing room for a longer run or a staging yard, classification yard, industrial area, or branch line.

Continuous Run Connector

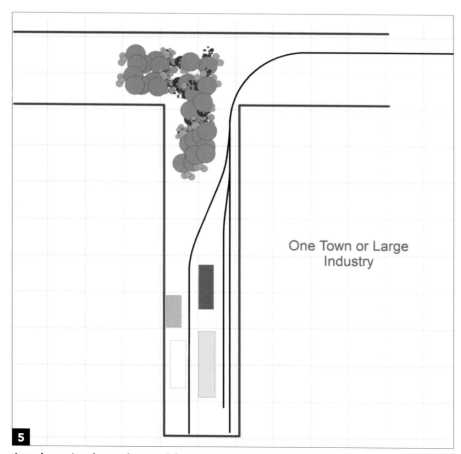

5

A stub peninsula can be used for a town, industry, or group of industries.

One Town or Large Industry

example. I'm assuming a common 18 x 20-foot space with access via a door (as opposed to stairs coming into the middle). Minimum radius is 30"; aisle widths are kept to 30" with the exception of a few pinch points. Let's see how things play out in each case.

Around the walls with one turn-back peninsula: For those that have the room, this design makes the most efficient use of space, **2**. It gives the longest "pure" mainline run length and offers the most badly needed linear runs.

Run length: 114 feet
Pros:
- Trains only pass through each scene once
- Operators can easily see, follow, and reach trains at all times
- Provides the maximum run length per square foot (taking into account ergonomics)
- Lends itself to punching through a wall and putting staging in an adjacent room if possible
- Long, straight runs will allow longer potential yards and towns

Con:
- Requires a lift-out bridge to cross the doorway

Around the walls, no peninsula: This is a very clean, open, easy-to-build design that's good for an industrial line, branch, or other prototype where a long mainline run isn't a primary goal, **3**. The shelf width can vary, and can comfortably be wider than with a peninsula.

Run length: 64 feet

Pros:
- Easy to build
- Very open design—leaves room in center of room for other (family) uses
- Continuous run

Cons:
- Shorter mainline run (only 56 percent of peninsula design)
- Requires lift-out bridge

Around the walls with a stub peninsula: This plan can be operated as a pure point-to-point, **4**, or, if you utilize the connector marked in purple, it offers continuous running. It's relatively easy to build and the center peninsula has a lot of operational and scenic potential while allowing wider aisles than the turn-back peninsula design. When running as a point-to-point operation the continuous run connector could be used as an industrial spur.

Run length: 80 feet

Pros:
- Easy to build
- Continuous run
- Open design

Cons:
- Lift-out required
- Moderate run length

Stub peninsulas: Stub peninsulas are extremely versatile, and can be used in a number of ways. You can have a single town, industry, or city scene, **5**, **6**. You can model two separate towns or industrial areas on either side of a center backdrop, **7**. You can use the peninsula as a stub-end classification or staging yard, **1**, **8**, or as a pair of stub-end staging yards, **9**. Without the burden of the space requirements of the peninsula curve, almost limitless possibilities exist to make highly effective use of the space operationally and scenically.

Before we move to the next variation, note that the any of the three designs we just covered could also be developed as point-to-point plans depending on your room shape, the format of your prototype, and what you're trying to accomplish.

6

Chuck Hitchcock used a stub peninsula to good effect in modeling his Kansas City Terminal Warehouse facility. *Keith Jordan*

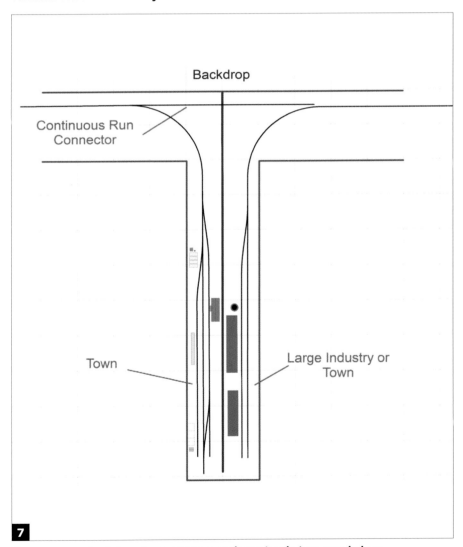

7

You can use a backdrop to separate a stub peninsula into two halves, resulting in two towns or industrial areas.

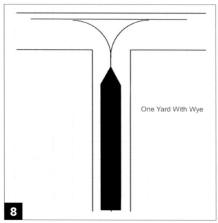

8

This stub peninsula houses a large single yard (staging or classification) including a wye.

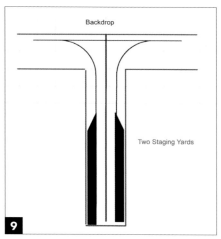

9

A stub peninsula can hold a pair of staging yards, with or without a center backdrop.

Around-the-walls "G" peninsula:
One of the more common spaces that modelers have available is the mid-sized spare bedroom. These are often large enough for a layout with a number of scenes. Many are large enough for some form of stub peninsula, but not large enough for a turn-back loop. Enter the highly versatile G-shaped layout, **10, 11.** Advantages include the lack of a lift-out bridge and that it lends itself particularly well to rooms with corner entrance doors.

Run length: 71 feet
Pros:
• No lift-out
• Easy to build
• Works well in rooms with a corner entrance door

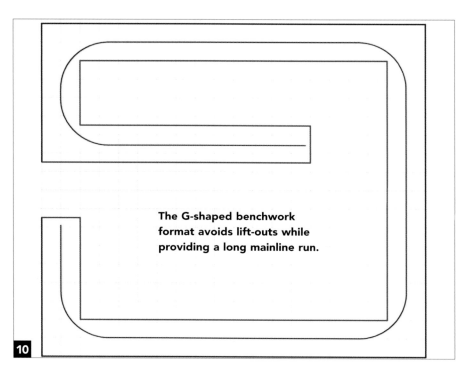

The G-shaped benchwork format avoids lift-outs while providing a long mainline run.

10

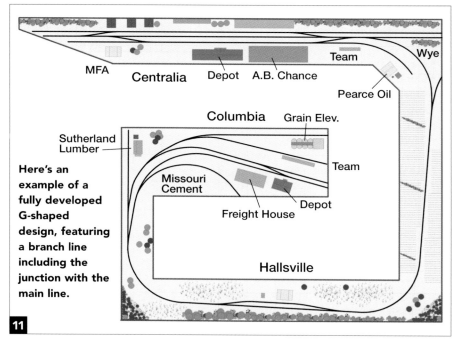

Here's an example of a fully developed G-shaped design, featuring a branch line including the junction with the main line.

11

Cons:
• No continuous running
• Shorter mainline run

Island: As the available space for a layout increases, the island format, with its many comfort and convenience advantages, becomes increasingly viable, **12**. Since it is free-standing, it easily clears all wall obstacles such as doors, windows, and utilities. It offers easy viewing access to all points since

it's not tight against the wall. There is no need for duckunders or lift-outs. It offers continuous running with walk around capability.

Run length: 72 feet
Pros:
• Trains only pass through a scene once
• No lift-out
• Provides a continuous run
• Operators can easily see and reach trains at all times

- Clears all wall obstacles

Cons:
- Generally provides the shortest run length
- Limited options for staging
- Limited long, straight runs

Dogbone: Folded-dogbone-style layouts (with a turnback curve at each end) were common in the early years of the hobby, largely as an alternative to a simple oval. I present the design here because it offers the longest mainline run of all the options and has the advantage of not requiring a lift-out, **13**. However, what's deceiving is that the quality of the run is less than desirable. There are so many compromises and downsides with this configuration that it's not my preferred design. The ergonomics and tight curves are less than ideal, particularly in HO and larger scales. The extra run length isn't that useful if you want to disguise the fact that a train passes through each scene twice. However, for the casual runner, having a train pass through a scene twice might actually be desirable.

Run length: 150 feet

Pros:
- Long mainline run
- No lift-out bridge

Cons:
- Long reach-in distances at corners
- Limited spots with long, linear runs
- Trains pass through each scene twice (hidden track is needed to disguise this)
- Hiding the return track (pink) increases ergonomic problems associated with hidden track

The case for only *one* peninsula

For many modelers a primary objective is to create the longest mainline run for their given space while at the same creating realistic-looking rights-of-way. Getting there can be tricky, though. Why? Not all run length is created equally—some is far more valuable and useful than others. Specifically, long linear runs are the most realistic and lend themselves best to laying out yards, towns, and industrial areas, **14**. Overlaying these key features on top of

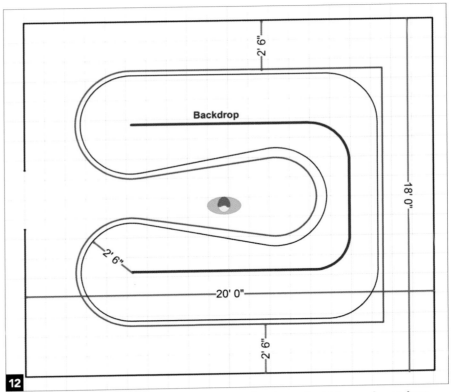

12

Island formats can be in a variety of shapes, the sizes of which are dependent upon the room length and width and the minimum radius.

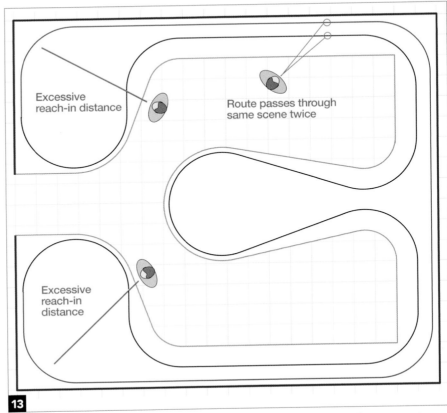

13

Dogbone formats avoid lift-outs and provide long mainline runs, but present problems with excessive reach-in distance in the corners and in hiding track that passes through scenes twice.

14

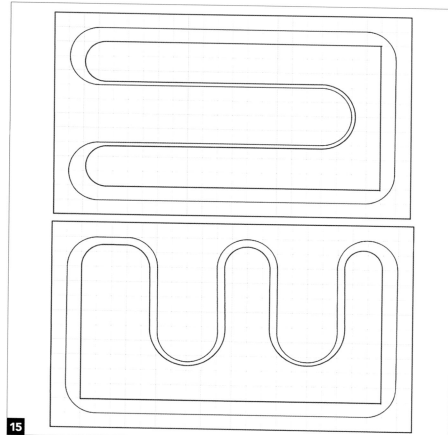

15

Plans with a single turnback peninsula, top, are always preferable to plans with multiple peninsulas, above.

The vast majority of prototype railroad right-of-way is linear. Capturing that look in our limited space is a challenge, to say the least!

curves is difficult—if not impossible—in many cases.

The bottom line is developing a plan that doesn't just create the maximum run length. Instead, we want a plan that creates the maximum *linear* run length. When that's the objective, the around-the-walls with one, and *only* one, peninsula is the most efficient.

The shortest distance between two points is a straight line. Of more importance, from a prototype railroad's point of view, it's generally the cheapest. As modelers, we have a disconnect between how the real world looks and the harsh reality that our layouts are located in rooms that dictate that all too frequently we hit the proverbial wall and must make a turn. We can't eliminate that problem, but there are design approaches that address the challenge more effectively than others. This is why the benchwork footprint, and its overlaid main line route, is one of the most important design decisions.

The more a design footprint

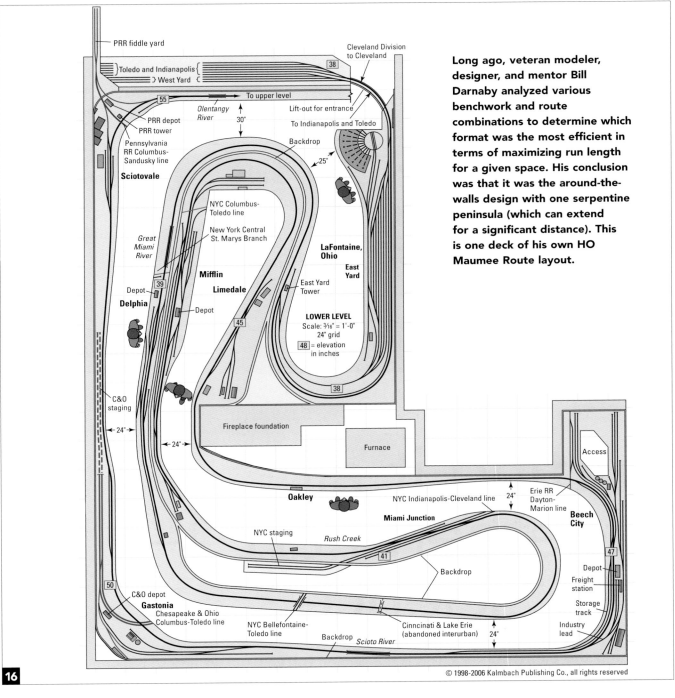

PRR fiddle yard

Toledo and Indianapolis
West Yard

Cleveland Division
to Cleveland

38

55

To upper level

Olentangy
River

30"

Lift-out for entrance

To Indianapolis and Toledo

PRR depot
PRR tower

Backdrop

Pennsylvania
RR Columbus-
Sandusky line

25"

Sciotovale

NYC Columbus-
Toledo line

New York Central
St. Marys Branch

**LaFontaine,
Ohio**

**East
Yard**

*Great
Miami
River*

Mifflin

East Yard
Tower

39

Limedale

Depot

45

LOWER LEVEL
Scale: ³⁄₁₆" = 1'-0"
24" grid

Depot

Delphia

Depot

48 = elevation
in inches

C&O
staging

38

24"

24"

Fireplace foundation

Furnace

Access

Oakley

NYC Indianapolis-Cleveland line

24"

Erie RR
Dayton-
Marion line

**Beech
City**

Miami Junction

NYC staging

Rush Creek

41

Backdrop

Depot

47

Freight
station

50

Storage
track

C&O depot

Gastonia
Chesapeake & Ohio
Columbus-Toledo line

NYC Bellefontaine-
Toledo line

Cincinnati & Lake Erie
(abandoned interurban)

24"

Industry
lead

Backdrop

Scioto River

Long ago, veteran modeler,
designer, and mentor Bill
Darnaby analyzed various
benchwork and route
combinations to determine which
format was the most efficient in
terms of maximizing run length
for a given space. His conclusion
was that it was the around-the-
walls design with one serpentine
peninsula (which can extend
for a significant distance). This
is one deck of his own HO
Maumee Route layout.

16

maximizes linear runs and minimizes curves, the more it lends itself to inserting the features we desire the most, such as yards, sidings, spurs, towns, and long bridges. Long, straight runs are prime: the more the better, and the longer the better. On the other side, 90- to 180-degree curves are very limiting: the fewer the better.

Many years ago Einstein (or maybe it was the Batavia club in Illinois—I can't remember) determined that the

most efficient use of a given space is an around-the-walls design with only *one* serpentine peninsula. This also assumes a pure plan, where the main line only passes through a scene once.

Let's take a look at an example to see why things shake out this way— for illustration purposes, let's assume a 14x24-foot room, **15**. Linear runs are shown in red; curves, in black. It shows that with the plan with multiple peninsulas, the quantity

and quality of your straight sections drops precipitously because so much of the run is spent getting into and out of curves. You can see a fully designed, large example of a single long peninsula in Bill Darnaby's HO Maumee Route, **16**.

Modeling the most common rail scenes is much easier the more long, linear runs of track we have. The around-the-walls format with *one* center peninsula provides that best.

1

CHAPTER SEVEN

Putting it all together: Part 1— the "science"

Arranging the elements on the canvas

Jim Six created this realistic, believable scene on his HO New York Central layout by following the prototype and allowing negative space between his structures. *Jim Six*

This is the section you've been waiting so patiently for, the one you thought would be the lead chapter, the X's and O's of creating a track plan. There's a reason it isn't first: When designs don't work, it usually has little to do with technical execution and everything to do with shortfalls in initial planning. We've gone over the strategic end. We've discussed how railroads work, the tools available to us, benchwork footprints, and route options. Now let's put it all together, **1**.

Since design formats are driven largely by room size and shape I'm going to go through some examples using the room configurations I most commonly see from my clients. As we go through these examples, there will be some degree of "back and forth" as we test various element locations and configurations. It's much like the scientific process: Start with an idea, test it, then refine.

In the last chapter, we discussed choosing around-the-walls or island benchwork, then choosing a route plan to overlay on the benchwork and sketching it in place. As a review, here's our continuing plan of attack for developing your ultimate design:

- Convert features (towns, yards, industries) from your prototype (or the prototype on which you're basing your freelance layout) to schematics and overlay them on the main line. Make sure to include scenery-only zones and negative space as placeholders
- Add secondary track
- Make several adjustment passes
- When the plan is complete, do a final "reality" self-check and ask yourself, "Can I build this?"

The "string-line" schematic

At this point we've nailed down at least a general sense of the benchwork footprint that works best, as well as the route configuration. That's major progress. Now we need to start planning for what elements will be placed along the route, their size, and—of vital importance—the spacing between these elements. Do you want larger, more realistic elements with ample space separating them, or do you want to compromise and have more (but smaller towns) with less distance between them? How you answer these questions will have a major impact both on appearance and in how operations "feel" in action.

Take a notepad and make a list of the elements you want featured on the layout. This includes specific towns and industries, industrial areas, specific structures, yards, and bridges. Include negative space (scenery-only zones) such as waterways, fields, valleys,

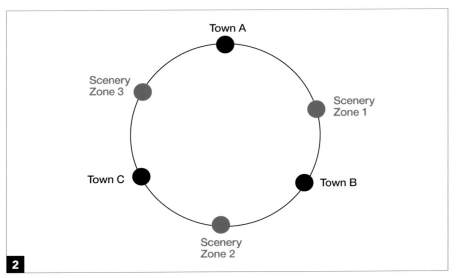

2

View the mainline route as a flexible necklace with each major element (town, yard, industrial park, negative space) represented by a bead. We have the flexibility to bend and twist the necklace, add or remove beads, and slide the beads around to change their spacing.

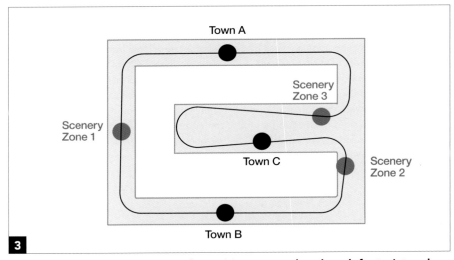

3

Overlay your "necklace" (route schematic) over your benchwork footprint and route diagram.

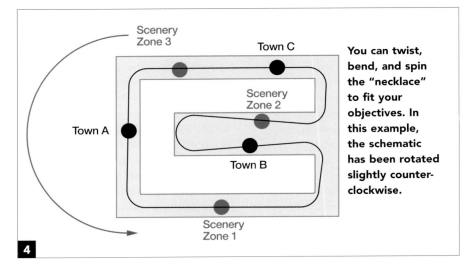

4

You can twist, bend, and spin the "necklace" to fit your objectives. In this example, the schematic has been rotated slightly counterclockwise.

Town and scene spacing
Or: How many towns should I put on my layout?

Early in the planning process, it's common for clients to tell me that they have a specific number of towns they'd like to have on their future layout but are having difficulty visualizing how to fit them all in. The simple answer is often because, in many cases, they simply won't fit!

Getting on a successful path with respect to model railroad layout design starts with zeroing in on the core questions that need to be asked. That's followed by having the self-awareness to give an honest answer to them. Finally, there are always tradeoffs—the final plan ultimately becomes an exercise in what is most important to you and what you're willing to give up in order to get it.

With respect to how many towns to include, the primary question is: Do you view the layout essentially as an operational chessboard where the sheer number of towns takes priority and appearance is of secondary importance? Or, do you want to capture the sense of a region visually, with appearance being important to you? Is watching trains wind through artistic and visually balanced scenes most important, or is maximizing track density for operations more important? When you can get a handle on the answer that fits your personal tastes, then you're on your way to deciding how many towns to aim for. How you go about reaching the final design boils down to the physical length of your towns *and* how much space you want between them. After that, it just becomes a matter of simple math.

If you view towns essentially as place-holders and don't need or care about a sense of distance, then a few feet of separation is all you need. However, if capturing the sense of an area is important then a second element needs to be incorporated: negative space to separate the scenes. Examples include fields, hills, mountains, wooded areas, vacant lots, and waterways. A scene separator creates a sense of distance either visually or in terms of actual distance or both. Without negative space, things take on the look of suburbia where one town abuts the next as opposed to going from town A to town B. That may be fine as long as you know what you're getting into going in.

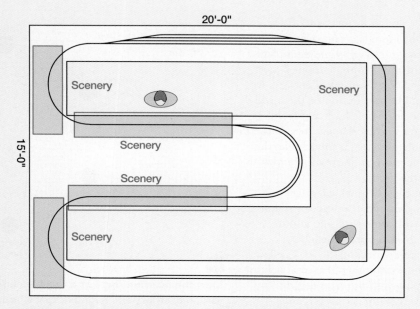

Placing the schematic over the route shows the emphasis on scenery and distance between towns

The planning process as it relates to how many towns you ultimately decide to incorporate (or can incorporate) comes down to three factors: the length of your mainline run, the physical length of your towns and yards (which is also driven by train length—do you want a long train to be entering town A while it is still passing through town B?), and how much space you allocate for scenery between towns. The accompanying drawings show how to approach planning the rough schematic,

with more-fully fleshed-out plans showing a more rural, open design versus a more tightly packed urban plan.

The fully developed plan below, of Jim Six's New York Central HO layout, shows many details we've discussed: an around-the-walls design with stub peninsula and lift-out bridge; separation among towns and scenic elements; varied shelf width; and a visible staging yard. (The photo on page 106 shows one town under construction.)

This fully fleshed-out plan shows how Jim Six opted to have fewer towns on his New York Central HO layout. Although there isn't a tremendous amount of space between them, he incorporated a lot of space between the structures and elements within each town. It's a great example of a fairly simple around-the-walls design with a short stub peninsula and a couple of additional benchwork bump-outs for key scenes.

Here are keys to keep in mind as you finalize your plan:

- Decide what's most important to *you*: maximizing the number of towns or incorporating fewer towns to allow room for scenery and a sense of distance. Prioritize what you're willing to give up in order to have the features that are most important to you.
- Sketch a schematic of your benchwork footprint and overlay a schematic of the main line run.
- Using actual yard ladder and turnout geometry (use actual track sections or photocopies of turnouts), rough out the length of your towns and yards.
- Place your "true to scale" town track geometry over the mainline schematic and adjust as needed until you have the look you are striving for.

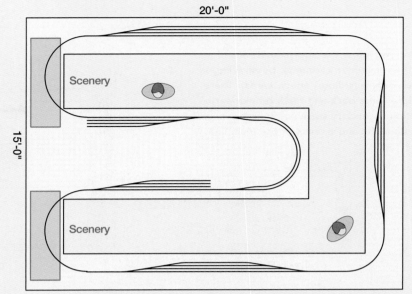

20'-0"

15'-0"

Scenery

Scenery

Here's an alternative plan geared for a modeler who wants to maximize the number of towns and place less importance on scenery and the separation between towns.

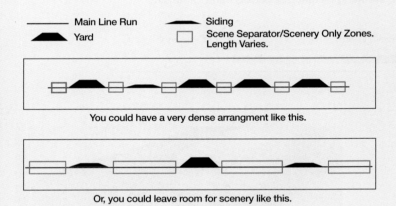

——— Main Line Run

◣ Yard

◣ Siding

☐ Scene Separator/Scenery Only Zones. Length Varies.

You could have a very dense arrangment like this.

Or, you could leave room for scenery like this.

Unfortunately you can't have 80 feet of "towns" on a layout with a 65-foot mainline run (top)! Increasing the negative space and eliminating a couple of towns gives us a workable starting point (bottom).

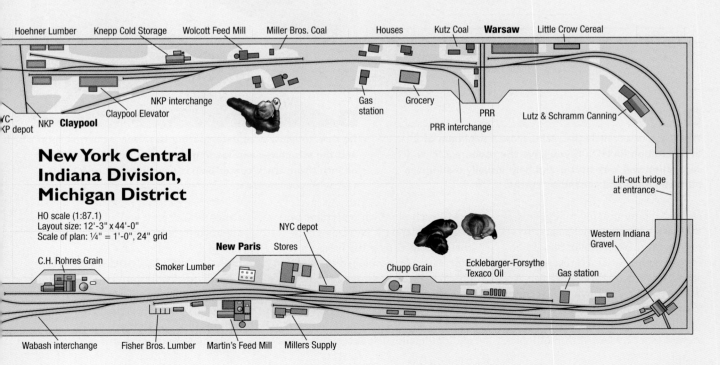

Hoehner Lumber   Knepp Cold Storage   Wolcott Feed Mill   Miller Bros. Coal   Houses   Kutz Coal   **Warsaw**   Little Crow Cereal

NKP interchange

Claypool Elevator

Gas station   Grocery

PRR

Lutz & Schramm Canning

NYC-NKP depot   NKP   **Claypool**

PRR interchange

New York Central Indiana Division, Michigan District

HO scale (1:87.1)
Layout size: 12'-3" x 44'-0"
Scale of plan: ¼" = 1'-0", 24" grid

C.H. Rohres Grain

Smoker Lumber

New Paris   Stores

NYC depot

Chupp Grain

Eckelbarger-Forsythe Texaco Oil

Gas station

Lift-out bridge at entrance

Western Indiana Gravel

Wabash interchange   Fisher Bros. Lumber   Martin's Feed Mill   Millers Supply

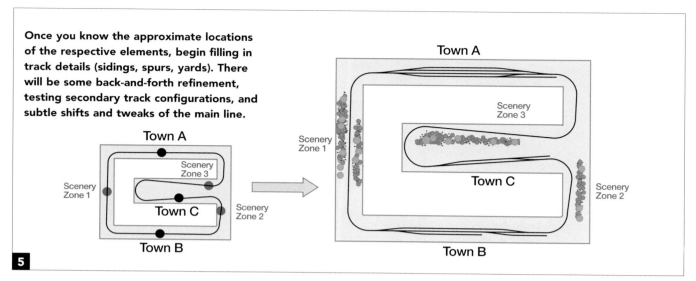

Once you know the approximate locations of the respective elements, begin filling in track details (sidings, spurs, yards). There will be some back-and-forth refinement, testing secondary track configurations, and subtle shifts and tweaks of the main line.

Town A

Scenery Zone 3

Scenery Zone 1

Town C

Scenery Zone 2

Town B

5

Town A

Scenery Zone 3

Scenery Zone 1

Town C

Scenery Zone 2

Town B

Adequate siding length is a tactical planning issue. Make sure you have enough length between clearance points to accommodate your typical train, including locomotive consists and caboose.

Clearance Point   Train Length   Clearance Point

2" parallel track spacing

6

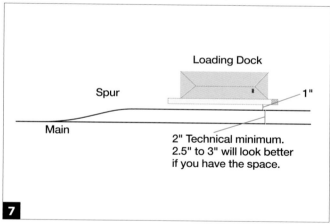

Loading Dock

Spur

1"

Main

2" Technical minimum.
2.5" to 3" will look better
if you have the space.

7

When a spur parallels the main, allow a minimum of 2" of separation (in HO). If you have the room, a 2.5" to 3" separation will look better and help visually distinguish between main and secondary tracks.

8

Be sure to allow adequate spacing between industrial spurs and the structures and loading platforms they serve. About an inch (from track center line) is usually good in HO, but test with your models.

---

forests, and mountains to separate the towns. If you model a specific prototype, these elements should be in geographic order. For example, one string-line list might read: Town A—Scenery Zone 1—Town B—Scenery Zone 2—Town C—Scenery Zone 3.

This order of elements can be viewed as a necklace with multiple beads, each of which represents one of the elements, **2**. Next, overlay this "necklace" over the basic route schematic you developed in the last chapter, **3**. You can rotate the necklace and adjust the spacing between elements until they fit the space the way you want, **4**. The next step will be adding details such as secondary track,

structures, scenery, and adjusting track alignments, **5**.

Developing secondary track

I divide trackwork into two categories: mainline and secondary track. Secondary includes sidings, spurs, industrial parks, and locomotive facilities—anything that is not on the

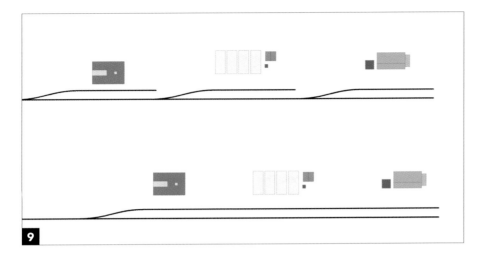

9

You can have a dedicated spur for each individual industry (top). However, with smaller industries on low-traffic lines it was common to have several industries on one spur (bottom). Either is correct. One spur means less track, fewer turnouts, and lower cost.

main line. Most of this book thus far has focused on the main line, since the position of the main drives the overall design. Its location is less flexible and its form dictates what type of layout we have regardless of style (point-to-point, continuous run, return loops).

Although secondary track involves far more volume in terms of turnout count (and possibly track length), its location is far more flexible. Its ultimate placement can, and probably should, be considered as "suggested placeholders." Not only can exact track location be considered a "game-time decision," even after construction, its very nature is such that removing and relocating secondary track isn't that difficult.

A key factor is how secondary trackage dovetails with the industries and structures it will serve. Layout construction often spans years, and it is likely you won't know exactly what structures—or even industries—you will ultimately be using at many locations.

Remember that design is a bit of a back-and-forth process: Although the main line drives things as you plan its location, you have to have at least a general sense of where the secondary track will likely be placed.

Remember to follow spacing minimums discussed in earlier chapters: 3" offset between the front-most track and the fascia (more if possible) and 3" minimum between the deepest track and the backdrop.

Be sure to allow adequate zones/space for your future structures. Going

in you may only have a general sense of how a town or industrial park may ultimately fill out. That's OK—just have in the back of your mind a general sense of the size of likely kits or scratchbuilt structures.

Also allow adequate parallel track spacing and clearance spacing for passenger platforms, freight platforms (and industry structures), locomotive shed doors, bridges, and other details.

Sidings and spurs: Their exact number and location will depend on your operational scheme. Make sure the lengths of the crucial passing sidings (as opposed to simple runaround tracks in industrial areas) will hold your most common train length (with locomotives and caboose), **6**. Make sure spurs and sidings are at least the minimum distance from the main (industrial spurs can be farther or at angles, **7**, **8**. At each location, you can use separate spurs to serve multiple industries, or use one spur, **9**.

Runarounds: Generally even the most basic branchline plan will need at least one runaround at the end of the line so that locomotives can run around the train to perform their work. As the size of your layout and the number of industrial zones and towns increases, so will the number of needed runarounds for switching moves. Do a mental run-through of how you'll operate and switch the layout to check yourself to make sure you have enough. Seek outside guidance as well: There are many professional railroaders in the hobby on various forums that are extremely generous with their time.

Since they run real trains for a living, their advice can be really helpful.

Maps: Maps of prototype railroads, including local maps and schematic drawings showing specific trackwork, can be extremely helpful as a guide to how track should be laid out. If you're a freelance modeler, find a prototype that is similar to your scheme and era.

Although there's an infinite number of ways secondary track could be designed, let's walk through an example of a moderately busy branch line with large towns at each end, **10**. Trains will include a dedicated eastbound and westbound local and perhaps some light passenger traffic.

Start by sketching a rough footprint of scenery, town, and building zones along the main line track. We know we want a passing siding in the middle, and a runaround track at each end, so we sketch those in. Let's now add a small classification yard at Town A, which we'll make the primary rail center. We'll also add a smaller yard at B, along with escape tracks (crossovers) to allow separating locomotives from inbound trains. Next, we add industries and spurs to give local freights some work to do. We can also then add details of structures and scenic details.

This is how planning progresses for the whole layout. Continue to work town by town, feature by feature, playing with different track arrangements until you find one that works for you.

Pulling it all together

Let's pull together all we've learned thus far into an actual, full-fledged, fully developed track plan. We'll walk through two examples based on the room sizes I most commonly see from my clients: a large spare bedroom (11 x 16 feet) and a typical 20 x 40-foot basement.

As we work through these examples

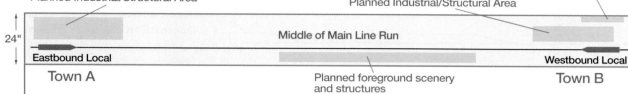

Planned "Tallish, 2 Story"
Background Structure

Planned Industrial/Structural Area

Planned Industrial/Structural Area

24"

Middle of Main Line Run

Eastbound Local

Westbound Local

Town A

Town B

Planned foreground scenery
and structures

Start by sketching the footprint of the zones for the key features. This represents a long stretch of line (the length is not to scale). We'll need industries to work at both ends, so block out an area for that. Let's also assume you want to plan for some scenery and/or structures and industries in the foreground and a taller structure against the backdrop.

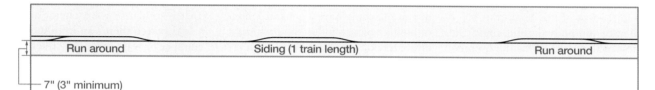

Run around

Siding (1 train length)

Run around

7" (3" minimum)

Let's add a 7" buffer between the front-most track and the fascia. Draw the main line in. Because of the run length, we will need a passing siding in the middle and runarounds at Towns A and B. Trains can now run end to end simultaneously, and have a way to pass one another mid-run. We've added a means for the locomotives to "escape" and run around their trains at each terminal town.

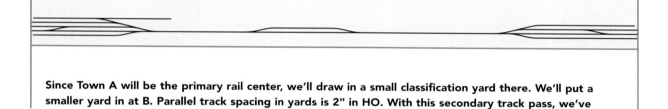

Since Town A will be the primary rail center, we'll draw in a small classification yard there. We'll put a smaller yard in at B. Parallel track spacing in yards is 2" in HO. With this secondary track pass, we've added the ability to sort and classify cars in preparation for their final destinations.

"Tallish, 2 Story"
Background Structure

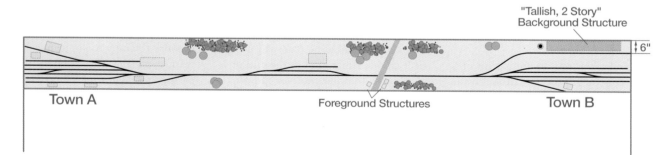

6"

Town A

Foreground Structures

Town B

The final pass provides industries to switch. What we want to do is roughly sketch in an initial, reasonable plan allowing space for structures we might expect to use. We can easily change this at any time (including after you've laid much of the track). Note that in the upper right corner of town B we have a tall structure against the backdrop. Tall, thin building flats tight against a backdrop can be unsightly. To improve the look, let's make the background structure slightly deeper and offset the spur 6" from the wall.

10

you'll see a common approach, which is to let the benchwork drive the design and, with the exception of the island style, making the key decision as to whether you want to have a center peninsula (and if so, which style).

Visualize as you go: As you work through your design it's important to check yourself from time to time. You alone will likely be building and interacting with the design that you draw. It's all too easy to get caught up in the enthusiasm of the moment and dismiss compromises as being no big deal, when often they are, in fact, a *very* big deal.

Consistently ask yourself: Do I have the skills to build this design? Would I enjoy building it? How much of the layout do I want to have finished after a year or so? Can I realistically do that, or are things getting too complex?

Comfort also matters. Ask: Can I easily reach all of the track? Can I comfortably reach all areas I'll need to scenic? Are the aisles wide enough? How do I feel about lift-outs and duckunders?

While the design process is mostly one of logical steps, don't fall into the trap of thinking it's an entirely linear path of step 1, step 2, step 3, and so on. There will be some back-and-forth refinement until you hone in on the final result. Even when you're satisfied with something on paper, you aren't completely done. A design is a "guide," a starting point. Once you get the benchwork up and see things in front of you in 3D form, you'll almost always see more refinements to be made, ideas to add, and track to modify.

The point is that the paper plan is something to keep you out of trouble and get you started. It doesn't have to be perfect: Be wary of falling into the common trap of "analysis by paralysis," which I've seen hold up more than one modeler for years (or even decades).

The spare bedroom

Let's start with the spare bedroom. In many cases clients have larger spaces elsewhere in their homes but, with increased experience, chose the smaller room to control the scope of what they bite off. This is a real example based on

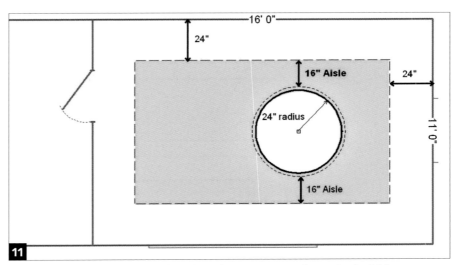

Start by lining the walls with benchwork: 24" is a good standard width to start with, but you can adjust areas to be narrower. Check the fit for various peninsula options. The template here shows there really isn't enough aisle width for a turn-back loop, so we'll go to a stub-end peninsula.

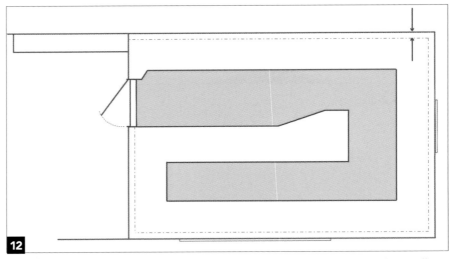

We've edited the plan to a G shape with lift-out, a stub peninsula, and a small staging area in the neighboring room. Establish a 4" (or more) buffer zone off of the wall to allow room for scenery and structures.

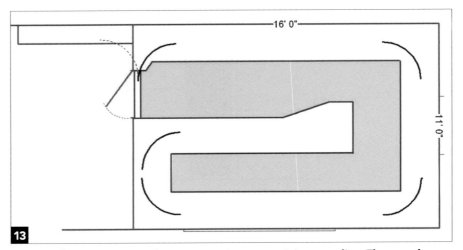

Draw in the curve arcs at the corners using your minimum radius. They can be shifted a bit based on whether you want the main nearer the backdrop or fascia.

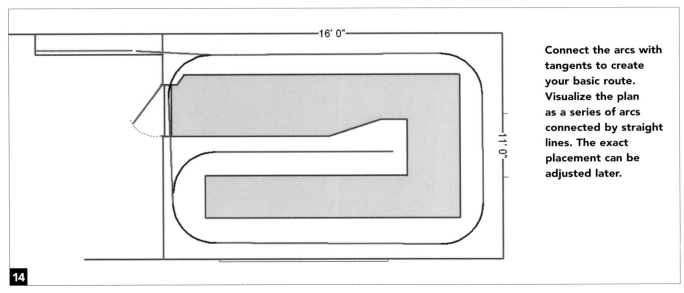

Connect the arcs with tangents to create your basic route. Visualize the plan as a series of arcs connected by straight lines. The exact placement can be adjusted later.

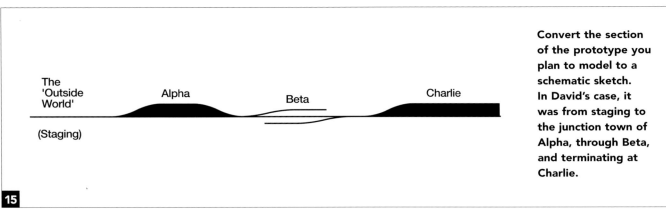

Convert the section of the prototype you plan to model to a schematic sketch. In David's case, it was from staging to the junction town of Alpha, through Beta, and terminating at Charlie.

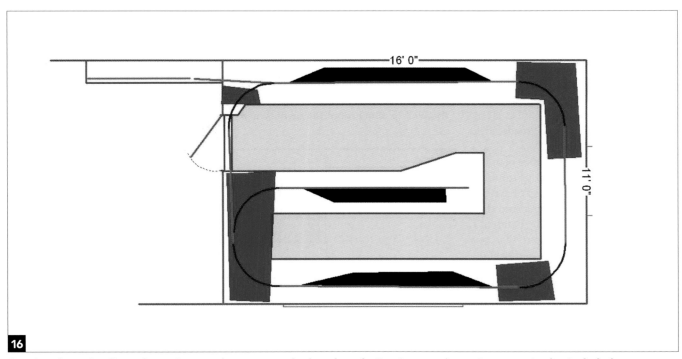

Overlay the string-line schematic atop the route on the benchwork. Scenic zones/negative space is also included.

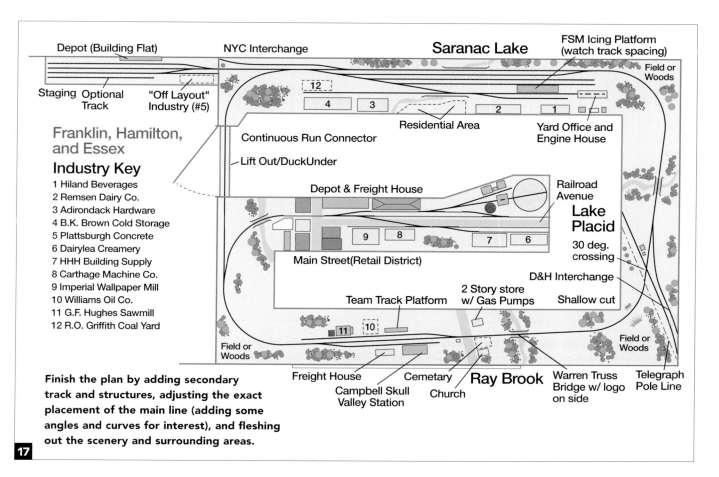

Depot (Building Flat) NYC Interchange **Saranac Lake** FSM Icing Platform (watch track spacing)

Field or Woods

Staging Optional Track "Off Layout" Industry (#5)

Residential Area

Yard Office and Engine House

Franklin, Hamilton, and Essex

Industry Key

1 Hiland Beverages
2 Remsen Dairy Co.
3 Adirondack Hardware
4 B.K. Brown Cold Storage
5 Plattsburgh Concrete
6 Dairylea Creamery
7 HHH Building Supply
8 Carthage Machine Co.
9 Imperial Wallpaper Mill
10 Williams Oil Co.
11 G.F. Hughes Sawmill
12 R.O. Griffith Coal Yard

Continuous Run Connector

Lift Out/DuckUnder

Depot & Freight House

Railroad Avenue

Lake Placid

30 deg. crossing

D&H Interchange

Shallow cut

Main Street(Retail District)

Team Track Platform

2 Story store w/ Gas Pumps

Field or Woods

Field or Woods

Freight House Cemetary **Ray Brook** Warren Truss Bridge w/ logo on side Telegraph Pole Line

Campbell Skull Valley Station Church

Finish the plan by adding secondary track and structures, adjusting the exact placement of the main line (adding some angles and curves for interest), and fleshing out the scenery and surrounding areas.

17

18

Here's a view of David's finished layout. It fits comfortably in his room, is realistic, and provides ample operational opportunities. *David Gallaway*

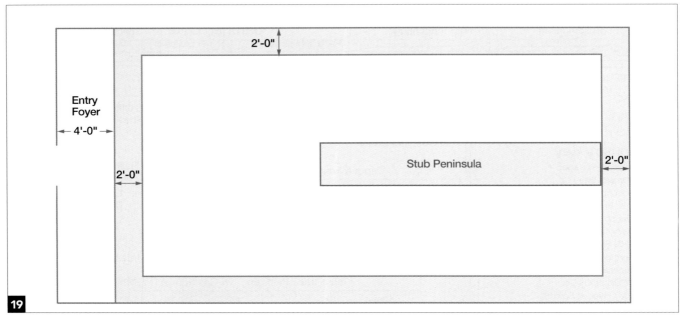

19

Begin by bordering the walls with benchwork 2 feet wide. We have plenty of space, so I added a wide 4-foot entry foyer. You could scale back on the scope and construction time by narrowing the shelves to 18" (or even 12"). However, maintain the full 24" width for benchwork adjacent to the foyer because a lift-out bridge will need the stability. Decide if you want a peninsula: You have plenty of room, as the simple stub peninsula outline shows.

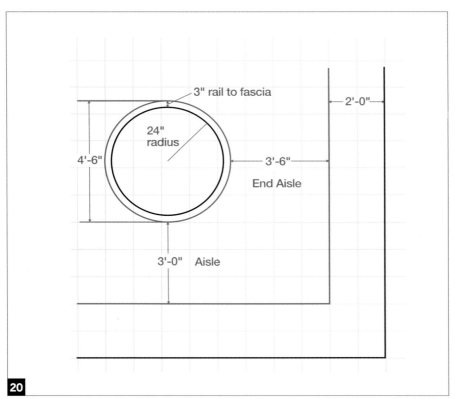

20

We'll assume that maximizing run length is the objective, so since we have room, we'll add *one* serpentine peninsula with a turnback loop at the end to maximize space (24" radius). The diameter of the turnback loop drives everything, so we'll need to start with locating that in the corner. Because of the size of the layout and the long linear runs of the benchwork, I've gone with minimum aisles of 36" and opened things up to 42" at the end.

New York Central's Saranac Branch. It was ultimately built in HO by Australian client David Gallaway.

Here was the design sequence: Start by bordering the walls with benchwork in the 18" to 24" range, **11**. Determine whether there's room for a turnback peninsula. In this case, with 24" minimum radius, by placing a circle in the plan we can see there's not enough room. We'll opt for a stub peninsula instead, **12**, also marking a 4" no-track zone around the walls/backdrop, adding a small shelf in the neighboring room for staging, and a lift-out section in front of the entry door.

Using your minimum radius, draw arcs at curve locations in the plan, **13**. Connect the arcs (blue) with tangent track (red), **14**, to establish the basic route. The plan is a basic point to point, with the lift-out allowing the option of continuous running.

In the meantime, we've taken our prototype (or freelanced versions of elements)—in this case, David's choice of the NYC branch—and converted it to a basic string-line schematic, **15**. It's a fairly simple branchline operation: a staging yard representing an outside connection, a large town (Alpha), negative space, a small town (Beta),

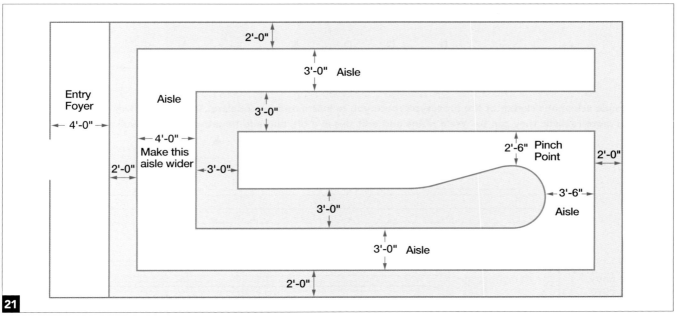

21 With the turn-back loop located, we can now draw in the rest of the peninsula. Aisle width was given priority over benchwork width. There's a narrow pinch point near the peninsula, but we'll be OK since it's short and the aisle opens up on each side.

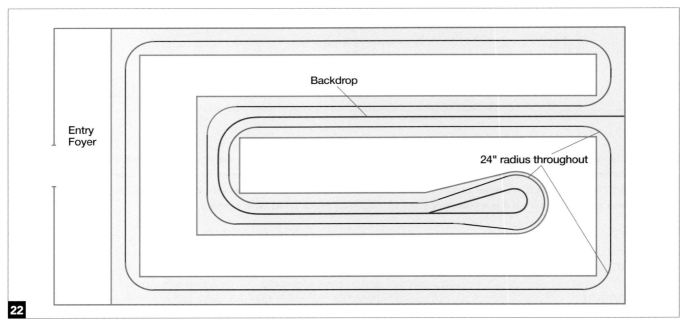

22 Let's insert a backdrop down the center of the peninsula to separate scenes. Now, sketch the mainline route, making sure not to encroach on the "no track" zones near the fascia or backdrop. We're assuming a 24" minimum radius. At this point the main thing is to get the route on paper. Later we can adjust the offset from the fascia, add curves, and add secondary track and other details.

negative space, and a terminal town (Charlie).

We now take that schematic and overlay it onto the basic route plan we've already sketched on the room plan, **16**. Negative space (scenic areas) is shown in green. We can then add secondary track, including a small yard

at Alpha, a turntable and runaround track at Charlie, and industrial tracks at all three, **17**. I adjusted the straight track in several areas so it doesn't always parallel the fascia.

We also added an interchange with another railroad between Alpha and Beta—the crossing is a dummy, but

the interchange track is live, effectively giving us another industry (one that can serve almost any kind of car). Various scenic elements finish the basic plan, including structures, a couple of waterways with bridges, streets, roads, trees, and fields.

You can continue revising the final

117

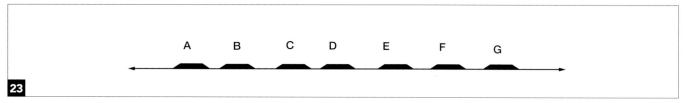

23 Draw a simple schematic sketch of the prototype route you're interested in modeling. The fewer towns you have, the larger and more realistic they can be. We'll refine and edit this in a bit, and add negative space as well.

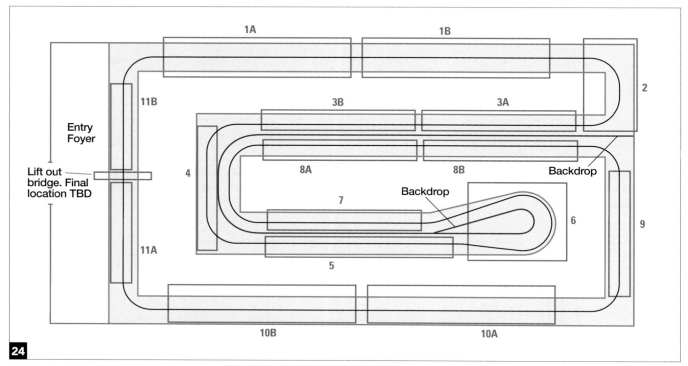

24 Divide the layout into "element zones." These are logical areas that could contain major elements such as a yard, siding, town, or scenic feature. For longer runs you have the choice of having one large zone or breaking it into two smaller ones (e.g. 1A and 1B). On the left we need to set aside a location for the lift-out bridge—we can adjust its final location later. Each element zone will contain a man-made feature or negative space filled with scenery.

details and track arrangements through construction. David's finished layout is shown in **18**.

Full basement

The second most common situation I see is the full or half basement, where somebody wants to have a large (but not enormous) layout. Let's look at developing a plan for that shape, based on my own basement. As we walk through the steps, a consistent theme will be "just because you can, doesn't mean you should." As you refine your design, it's a good idea to frequently do a mental walk-through of the work involved in building it and compare that against your available time.

Be aware of over-reaching—trying to incorporate more elements than your available square footage will allow (visually or mechanically). This is a primary design error and is the difference between an end result that looks like a model of a railroad as opposed to a toy train set.

Start with a basic footprint of the layout space—in this case, 20 x 40 feet with an entry door centered on one end. As **19** shows, since we have a lot of space I added a 4-foot entry foyer and added a 24"-wide shelf around the perimeter. We can always narrow the benchwork in some areas later if needed, but let's start with wide benchwork and see how things progress.

We now need to make the critical decision regarding a peninsula. We have

plenty of room, as the sketch shows with a simple stub peninsula. For many modelers, a 20 x 36 around-the-walls design will provide more than enough mainline run, with ample room for all the layout features they desire. Such a design would be easy to build and progress would be relatively quick. That option also allows using the center of the room for many other purposes (lounge, TV area, workbench, etc.).

The simplest peninsula option would be a basic stub version as shown, which could be used for staging, a branch line, or industrial area. If the no-peninsula or small stub peninsula options provide what you need, stop here and go directly to developing your schematic.

If, however, you're an operator and want to maximize your mainline run, including several towns, we'll proceed to the next option: a single long end-loop peninsula. In **20**, we're overlaying the minimum radius (in this case, 24" for a transition-era layout using mainly 40- and 50-foot cars) return loop on a corner of basement/benchwork outline. Doing so shows that we have enough room for a 3-foot-wide peninsula with 3-foot aisles (with a smaller pinch point), **21**.

To keep the scenes on the peninsula "pure," let's add a view block/backdrop down the full length of its center, **22**. We can then sketch the basic mainline

route on the whole layout. Don't worry about towns, yards, or other details—just get the basic route in place.

Sketch a basic schematic of your prototype main line (or freelanced route), including towns, interchanges, and other features you'd like to include, **23**. This will mean specific towns if you're following a prototype, or towns pulled from various sources if you're freelancing.

Divide the layout plan into "element zones," areas that could feature a town, scenic element, yard, or negative space, **24**. I went back to the track schematic and narrowed it down to four towns/cities/yards that I felt could be

comfortably included on the plan, **25**, and laid that trimmed-down schematic atop the route plan, **26**. This is purely a judgment call. Could we have worked another town into the plan? Possibly, but at the cost of a cramped plan with less negative space, and the risk of having a train with its locomotive in one town and caboose in another.

Developing a final plan

Now, let's set a strategy for adding the secondary track. Let's assume the theme of a small Class 1 railroad in the late 1950s and an interest in having formal operating sessions.

We'll need passing sidings—10-foot-long sidings are long enough for two four-axle locomotives, 15 40-foot cars, and a caboose. We'll also put yards at Towns C and F, making sure they're not the same size.

When doling out operating assignments, by far the most popular are locals and yard jobs. This means we need to design enough operational interest for at least one local freight going each way. Let's also add one dedicated large-industry job. Multi-spot industries pack in a lot more operational

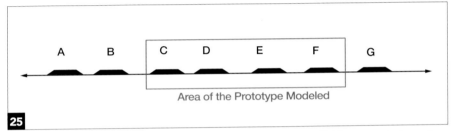

25

Going back to our schematic and looking at the zones available to us, let's make an "executive" decision to model four of the prototype's online elements. Is there a formula to determine this number? Unfortunately, no. It's an aesthetic decision that will involve some trial and error on paper.

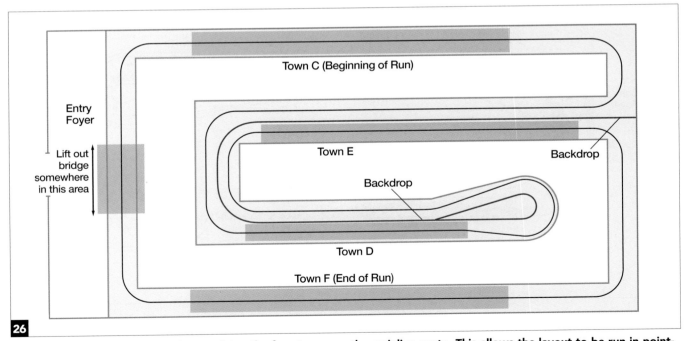

26

Overlay the string-line schematic containing the four towns on the mainline route. This allows the layout to be run in point-to-point fashion starting at Town C, traversing the mid-section of the layout and terminating at F. Having D directly across the aisle from F isn't perfect, but we'll live with it as a compromise to keep the towns equidistant. We've created zones or boxes for the towns, concentrated our man-made elements within those zones, and been self-disciplined about not encroaching on negative space. We can tightly pack the individual towns with plenty of operational interest.

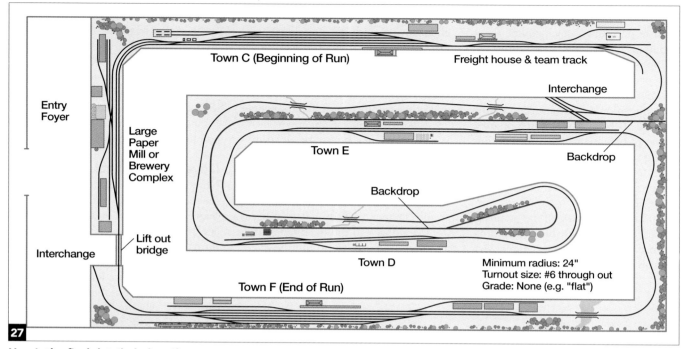

27

Here's the final detailed plan. If you are an "operator," staging could be handled in one of two ways. First, you could simply view towns C and F, with their adequate yards, as staging yards. As long as you're dealing with a modest volume of trains this could be viable. This type of room often has utility rooms and workshops to what would be the left of the drawing. If this were your situation, you could punch through a wall into those rooms and put staging on shelves.

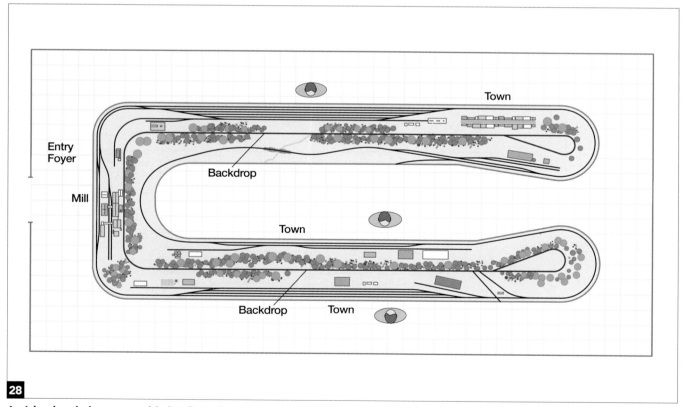

28

An island-style layout would also fit in the same space. The mainline run is shorter, but there's no need for a lift-out bridge.

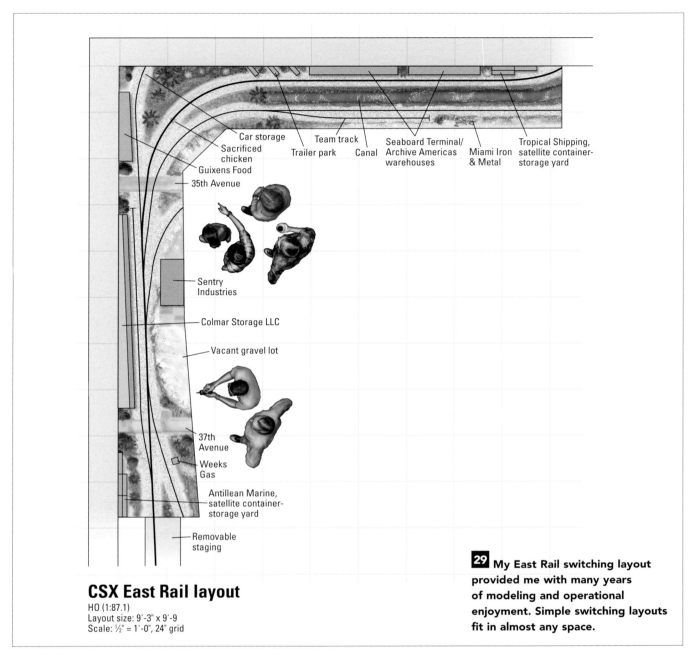

Car storage
Sacrificed
chicken
Guixens Food
35th Avenue
Trailer park   Team track   Canal
Seaboard Terminal/
Archive Americas
warehouses
Miami Iron
& Metal
Tropical Shipping,
satellite container-
storage yard

Sentry
Industries

Colmar Storage LLC

Vacant gravel lot

37th
Avenue

Weeks
Gas

Antillean Marine,
satellite container-
storage yard

Removable
staging

CSX East Rail layout

HO (1:87.1)
Layout size: 9'-3" x 9'-9
Scale: ½" = 1'-0", 24" grid

29 My East Rail switching layout
provided me with many years
of modeling and operational
enjoyment. Simple switching layouts
fit in almost any space.

play value per square foot than single-commodity industries like coal or grain, so that's what we'll do. The finished plan is shown in **27**.

Operationally one scenario will be:
• Yard Job (two operators)
• Mill Job (two operators)
• Local—out-and-back turn (two operators)
• Through freights/passenger trains (two operators, each handling trains in one direction)

During an operating session, the lift-out bridge would be removed and the layout operated as a true point-to-

point. The bridge will be used when the owner wants to just let the trains casually cruise. Trains will originate and terminate in the end-point yards. Another option would be to add staging yards on each end, possibly on shelves in the foyer area (or punching through to an adjoining room).

Let's take a quick look at the same room with an island-style plan, **29**. This is a viable option in a room this size. Although the main line run would be shorter and there's no option for additional staging, the island has the advantage of no duckunders/lift-

outs and doesn't interfere with wall obstacles such as doors and utilities.

Switching layouts

Many modelers—and it really is a large percentage—either don't have the time or space for even a spare-bedroom layout. Enter the shelf-style switching layout. These can be worked into the corner of almost any room. Don't underestimate the amount of enjoyment and satisfaction this format can provide in both construction and operation, **29**. The smaller size takes a lot of the pressure off in terms of

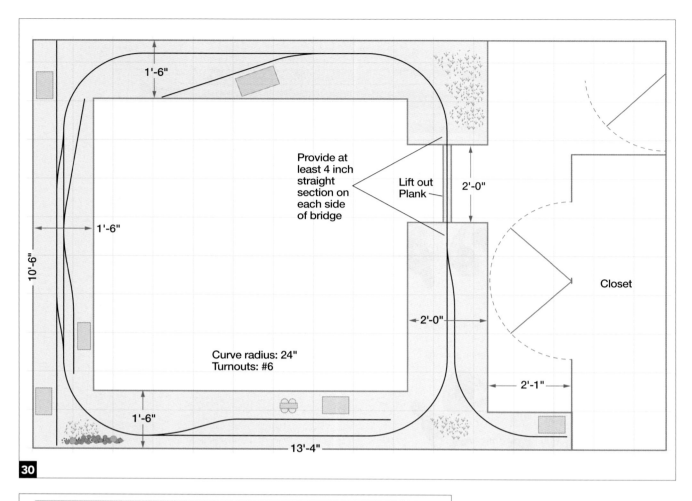

30

Provide at least 4 inch straight section on each side of bridge

Lift out Plank

1'-6"

1'-6"

10'-6"

2'-0"

2'-0"

Closet

Curve radius: 24"
Turnouts: #6

2'-1"

1'-6"

13'-4"

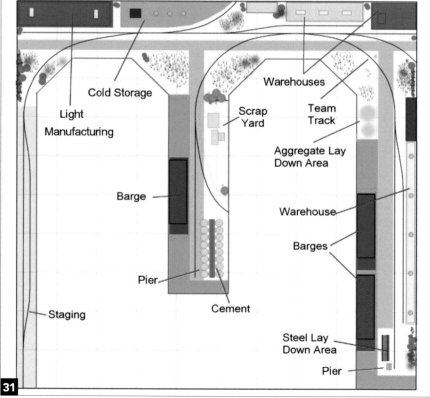

31

Cold Storage

Light Manufacturing

Scrap Yard

Warehouses

Team Track

Aggregate Lay Down Area

Barge

Warehouse

Pier

Barges

Cement

Staging

Steel Lay Down Area

Pier

Above: Here's a design for a small spare room, typical of an apartment, condo, or house bedroom.

Left: This port-themed switching layout would fit in a small room, with no lift-out section needed.

covering lots of surface area, and these layouts can be relatively inexpensive to build. The smaller size allows the owner to focus on extremely high levels of detail, is a good skills-building platform, and if operated prototypically can still spin off relatively significant operating sessions.

Another small layout option is a small room, such as an apartment second bedroom (which tend to be smaller than those in most houses). Let's look at a few plans for those spaces with a few guidelines: I've allowed 25" clearance in front of the closet doors, limited lift-out length to 24", and kept the benchwork width at 24" for stability (in an apartment we're

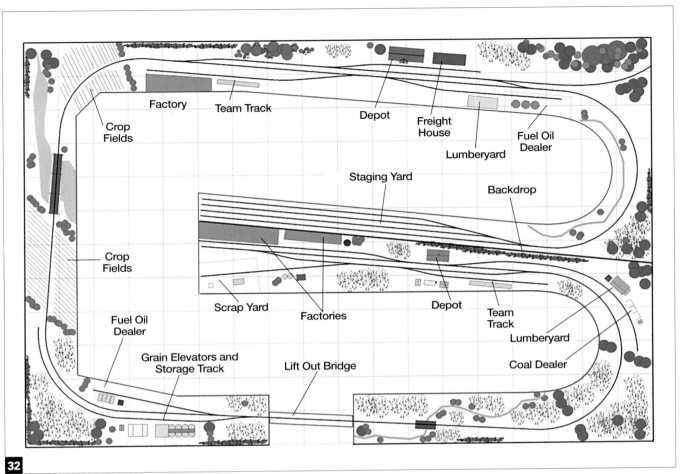

32

This plan captures the feel of a small Midwestern branch line. It's a fairly simple around-the-walls with a stub peninsula.

using free-standing benchwork instead of anchoring shelves to walls). The layout in **30** keeps the center of the room open (the benchwork could be bumped out in one or two areas). You can use peninsulas, **31**, **32**.

Remember the prototype

If you get stuck coming up with appropriate track configurations, remember that we are almost certainly modeling something that's been done in the real world. Somewhere, sometime a prototype railroad mechanical engineer came up with the track design solution. Check maps and schematic drawings (many railroading books include them, as do many railfan websites), and Google Earth views. If you aren't modeling a specific prototype, you can use these sources for almost any prototype railroad when looking for ideas.

The case for 1:1 planning

In many cases, especially where room size is modest, you don't even need a drawing. You'll likely know where the benchwork will go, so you can simply tape its outline on the floor and rough things out with track sections or more tape. You can also build the benchwork and follow the same approach, **33**. There are huge advantages to this "1:1 scale" design approach. Seeing things in front of you full-scale gives you a much more accurate sense for what the design will ultimately look like than when you do it on paper.

Even if you're planning a large layout, you can rough-in smaller scenes or towns with this approach (even setting some trains and structures in place) to get a feel for how the finished areas will look.

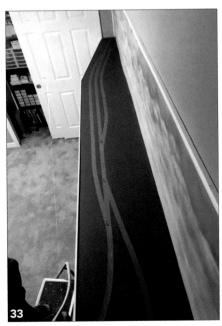

33

Veteran modeler Tom Johnson designed his layout using 1:1 mockups in lieu of a two-dimensional drawing. He then roughed in track locations atop the benchwork with tape.

Tom Johnson

1

CHAPTER EIGHT

Putting it all together: Part 2—the "art"

Balance, emphasis, and other visual keys to designing a realistic layout

This scene on my Downtown Spur layout illustrates how applying principles from the art world can add a further dimension to our hobby, transporting us to a specific place and time. Emphasizing key elements by surrounding them with mundane ones and using color to highlight key features are among the tools available to us.

We can be infinitely more effective in achieving a pleasing modeling result if we know the motivation behind it, the "why," before we fixate on how we'll get there. When we truly understand where our satisfaction comes from, we can then understand where the underlying motivation for achieving it springs. Only when we reach that point are we truly ready to identify the necessary steps to ultimately create something we are excited to be around.

In dealing with a tremendous variety of clients from varying backgrounds and experiences, I've spent a lot of time trying to understand what it is at the deepest level that brings them all together. What is it that makes model railroading so compelling for hundreds of thousands of people?

What I've come to realize is that ours is really not a hobby. It runs far deeper than that. What we do is far more aligned with the arts than the hobby world. When we come to that realization, we are finally in a position to attack our work from the proper perspective. Model railroading is a unique blend of viewing a painting, a sculpture, a masterful architectural work, and watching a great film—although unlike film we are active participants.

We are looking for the same experience we get from the arts. We want to be transported, inspired, and uplifted, **1**. As logical, technical, and procedural as layout design may seem at times, that can be deceiving. Beneath it all is an emotional drive. When you go to your layout room after a hard day

at work, grab the throttle, and interact with a successfully conceived model railroad, you enter another world and your mind drifts. You get carried away in exactly the same way as when you come out of a masterfully executed movie. It's the *experience* that compels us—not whether that curve radius is 24" instead of 26" or the window on the depot has 8 mullions instead of 12.

This might seem excessively deep or overwrought, but know that understanding this idea creates almost limitless opportunities. Why? Because if we correctly align our endeavors with the arts we open up the doors to vast resources of information that have been refined over the millennia. All we have to do is to take those time-developed theories from the art world and apply them. Just knowing and embracing that reality, that possibility, is the hard part. Stepping out from the modeling umbrella and taking art courses related to visual literacy and composition will, over the long term, greatly improve your overall designs.

A friend of mine made an offhand comment that created the perfect analogy for this section. He stated

that people fall into two categories: machinists and artists. This might be true to an extent, but those two perspectives aren't mutually exclusive. They can work in unity; it's not an either or situation. A design can be technically correct, totally functional, and by all measures perfectly acceptable—but be dull and lacking life. By applying art to architecture, we build on the functional design to create a far more fulfilling experience, **2**.

What we will be discussing in the pages ahead is a direct parallel. In the art world, things start with the visual elements: lines, shapes, textures, lightness vs. darkness (value), space, and color. The process and decisions we make to organize those elements is called design, the five principles of which are: unity and variety, balance, scale and proportion, emphasis and focal point, and rhythm.

Although I didn't call them that (I called them tools), we've already covered the visual elements that relate most to modeling. Applying them in a vacuum with a skilled machinist's viewpoint, we will likely end up with a technically correct, less-artistic plan

2 A good parallel for this chapter is a breathtaking architectural masterpiece such as the Puente de la Mujer bridge in Buenos Aires. The structure follows fundamentally sound engineering practices—the technical aspect that will get you from one side to the other. However, that technical foundation is overlaid with masterful architectural and artistic concepts, creating something truly magnificent. *Lance Mindheim collection*

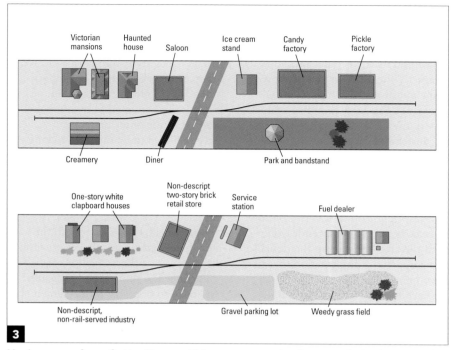

Victorian mansions · Haunted house · Saloon · Ice cream stand · Candy factory · Pickle factory · Creamery · Diner · Park and bandstand

One-story white clapboard houses · Non-descript two-story brick retail store · Service station · Fuel dealer · Non-descript, non-rail-served industry · Gravel parking lot · Weedy grass field

3

Having a number of attention-grabbing structures in close proximity (top) results in visual chaos, creating a scene that falls apart logically. It's better to surround key structures and elements with mundane, ordinary structures (lower).

typified by a more linear, grid-like look. Such plans are slightly easier to build than one that incorporates some artistic overlays.

Again, there is no shame in taking that route ... as long as it's a conscious decision and not for lack of awareness of the world beyond. If you're a beginner, or skew heavily to the chess game/operations end of the hobby, you may just want to go that route and stop there without guilt. If not, read on.

We'll cherry-pick the design concepts from the world of art and architecture that best apply to what we're doing, and see how they apply to model railroad layout design.

Unity and variety

Unity in artwork creates a sense of harmony and wholeness by using similar elements within the composition and placing them in a way that brings them all together. Variety adds interest by using contrasting

4

The focal point on my Los Angeles Junction layout is May-Vern Liquor, the triangular art deco structure in the foreground. It is emphasized by its location at the most prominent portion of the layout and its contrasting color.

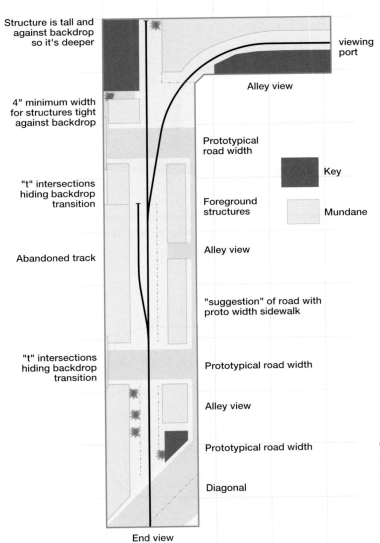

Structure is tall and against backdrop so it's deeper

4" minimum width for structures tight against backdrop

"t" intersections hiding backdrop transition

Abandoned track

"t" intersections hiding backdrop transition

viewing port

Alley view

Prototypical road width

Key

Foreground structures

Mundane

Alley view

"suggestion" of road with proto width sidewalk

Prototypical road width

Alley view

Prototypical road width

Diagonal

End view

On my LAJ layout I overemphasized mundane and low-lying structures (painted in muted pastels) to highlight the three focal-point structures.

5

In looking at this prototype scene, note that no individual elements hit you over the head with a visual sledgehammer. The structures are low-key and repetitive with no eye-grabbing details. The colors are muted and faded. It just looks "railroady."

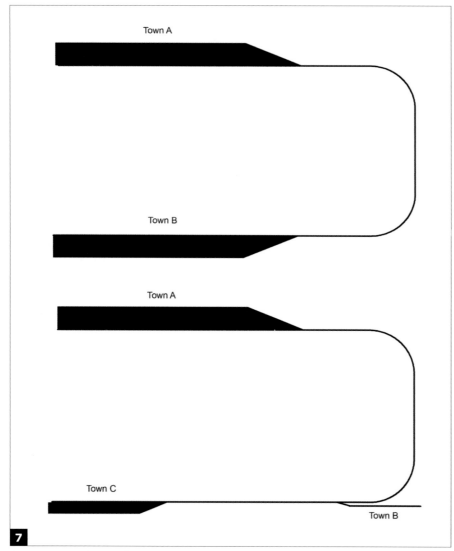

Town A

Town B

Town A

Town C

Town B

Symmetry applies to layouts as a whole. In the top schematic we have two equal-size towns symmetrically balanced on the layout. Contrast that to the more interesting asymmetrical balance on the bottom.

elements within the composition.

A quote from sophia.org explains it well: "Without unity, an image is chaotic and 'unreadable.' Without variety it is dull and uninteresting. Unity and variety in a composition are said to be the most important principles of design. This is because these two principles are what are needed to hold a composition together. Good design is achieved by a balance of these two principles. Elements within a composition need to be similar enough for us to perceive that they belong together, but different enough to be interesting. When a composition is unified, its different elements are all working together to support the design as a whole. Unity is whether a piece of art or a design is harmonious or cohesive. If you've ever heard of gestalt theory, this is where it comes in. Gestalt theory, stated simply, is that the whole is greater than the sum of its parts. (See inklingcreative.ink.)

Translating this to modeling, Tony Koester put it succinctly in his book *Planning Scenery For Your Model Railroad* (Kalmbach): "Some model railroads look more like a display of craftsman-style structure kits than a coherent miniature of any actual place and period. Any of the structures could have been a contest winner; seen as parts of a greater whole, however, they failed to do their jobs."

This simply means we must look at our layout as a whole, not at the

At top is a typical composition with an emphasis on 90-degree orientations. Operationally, there are no issues here, but visually something seems subtly "off"—it's a little too orderly. By taking the same elements and angling them (bottom), the scene becomes much more interesting. Angling streets and streams also makes it easier to hide troublesome layout-to-backdrop transition spots.

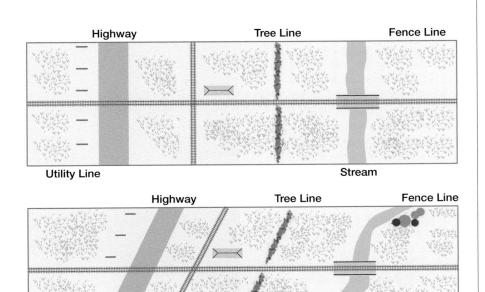

8

The same principle applies to tracks. A main line parallel to the fascia is the simplest to build and makes efficient use of the space. However, it suffers from a little too much symmetry. Angling the track adds visual interest. Whether you can do this depends on many factors, including prototype design, corner curves, and benchwork width.

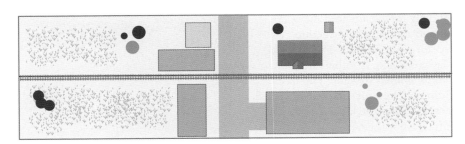

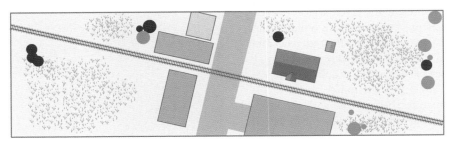

9

individual parts. If you have an eye-catching item in one place, you need to offset it with something mundane elsewhere or else you will have visual chaos. Every component should have a role. It can be a supporting role, or setting up another component, but it's still a role. Every element should be something we would reasonably expect to see in that setting.

Sooner rather than later in the planning process you need to decide which elements to place on your canvas—elements being man-made features such as structures, roadways, and bridges, along with natural features such as vegetation, hills, mountains, and rivers. Therein lies the trap that commonly ensnares railroad modelers. We say, "Here's my (often limited)

layout surface area. I've got structures A, B, C, and D that all look very cool. How do I squeeze, twist, turn and hammer them into my available space?" Or a variation: "The prototype scene I'm modeling has 12 structures. How do I fit them all in?" In either case, it's the proverbial situation of trying to fit 10 pounds of bolts in a 2-pound box, **3**.

Unfortunately, in many cases, we

actually do find a way to wedge them on the layout, then we step back and discover that something looks off, *really* off. This approach results in what I call the "catalog cover" or "amusement park" look. It's a caricature. It doesn't look like what we want, which is a "model of a railroad"—instead it looks like a toy train set. The misstep is in focusing on element selection and not putting enough space between the elements.

Prototype railroads and towns are typically a collection of a lot of common, mundane elements. It's what our eye is looking for in a model, whether we are consciously aware of it or not. In our zeal to fit all of the cool models in, we tend to subconsciously delete all of the mundane elements that were so crucial to "framing" the central subjects. We won the battle and lost the war.

Don't fall into the trap

I call this the trap of element-driven design, and I see it often with clients. The typical situation, especially for experienced modelers, is where accumulated structure inventory becomes the driving point of layout design. Another situation is undisciplined structure purchases driven only by a kit's individual appeal, whether or not the kits relate to any central layout theme.

It's very common for individuals to have life circumstances that for several years prevent them from building that first layout. In a totally understandable quest to stay engaged in the hobby they participate by acquiring and building models (rolling stock, structures, bridges), all with the intent of using everything on a future layout. I've known people who have done this for decades, and their resulting inventory is pretty massive. Some do this with a focused plan, but in many cases these models have accumulated with, at best, only a vague idea of a theme and size of a future layout.

When the day finally arrives that they can finally have that layout of their dreams, they look at their inventory (especially structures) and their first thought is how they can design a layout to accommodate all of

I used aesthetic, gentle S-curves on my Monon N scale layout. Large, sweeping curves create visual interest—provided that there's an apparent reason for them to be used (rivers, hills, and other scenic elements).

10

11

Prototype railroads use simple curves and S-curves to go around and through features such as lakes, hills, mountains, and rivers. *Jeff Wilson*

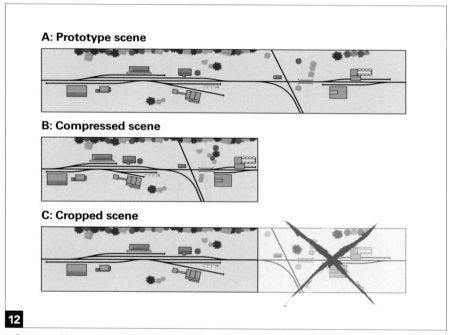

A: Prototype scene

B: Compressed scene

C: Cropped scene

12

When modeling an appealing scene (top), but lacking the proper space to do it justice, our natural tendency is to squeeze everything more tightly together so it fits (middle). However, by doing so we eliminate the needed negative space that created the pleasing effect of the scene in the first place. It's better to crop out some elements and maintain the spacing (bottom).

them. Without a central theme, you end up with a case of the tail wagging the design—the entire design process becomes trying to fit these often unrelated pieces. If left unchecked, the end result becomes a ping-pong table display of lots of structures with spurs in front of them, which is a mess of a layout design.

Emphasis/focal points/subordination:

As you look at your overall concept, it's likely that there are vignettes, scenes, and structures that you'd like to emphasize and draw attention to. A key is that in order for something to be "emphasized," by default its neighbor must be less so. Emphasis is defined as an area or object within the artwork that draws attention and becomes a focal point. "Subordination" is minimizing or toning down other compositional elements in order to bring attention to the focal point. The focal point refers to the area in a composition that has the most significance, an area that the artist wants to draw attention to as the most important aspect.

There are several ways we can emphasize a layout element. First is location: If you have a focal scene for the layout, ideally you'd like to place it where it's seen first when entering the room. Remember in Chapter 7 when we discussed the concept of reducing our track plan to a necklace with beads: Spin the necklace so the "prominent bead" is in the most advantageous viewing location, **4**.

Second is subordination. My friend Chuck Hitchcock said, "The key to instilling realism is to highlight the ordinary." That means downplaying the surrounding elements to highlight the key one.

Let's say, for example, you have a prominent depot. If you surround it with Victorian mansions and other attention getters, it won't be as noticeable as if its neighbors are several mundane, muted-tone warehouses, a parking lot, or a city block of ordinary brick buildings.

Next is element size. A large concrete grain elevator with 24 tall

13

Master modeler Tom Johnson is an artist by profession and it shows in the outstanding visual cohesiveness of his work. Note the ample amount of space between the elements—the rolling scenery emphasizes the structures—and the treatment of lines (track) in the scene. *Two photos: Tom Johnson*

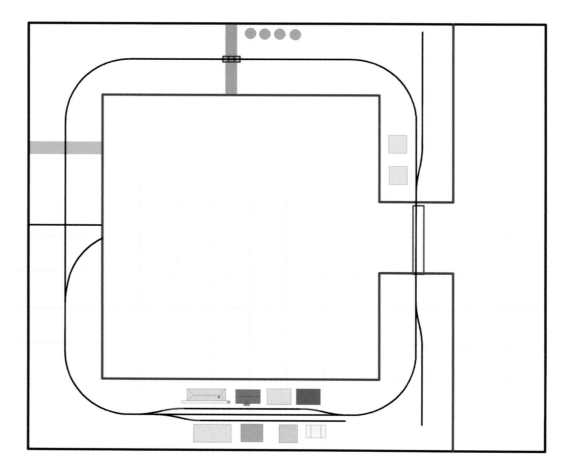

silos will obviously carry more visual emphasis and weight than a version with eight shorter silos or a small wooden 1920s-era elevator.

The final way to emphasize an element is color. A brighter, more-saturated subject will stand out in a background of muted tones, **5**.

Work hard to blend signature elements and mundane elements, remembering that by downplaying the elements neighboring our focal points, we emphasize the main subject. By making extensive use of mundane elements, making them the majority, we will create contrast, highlighting the things to which we want to draw attention, **6**.

Mundane elements are the ordinary scenic features and structures found in droves in the real world; things that don't catch the eye. Examples include nondescript warehouses (brick, concrete, or painted in muted tones), vacant lots, parking lots, brick storefront buildings, plain white clapboard houses, small dry creekbeds and ditches, farm fields, sheds, groups of trees, and utility structures.

Steep the balance in favor of the mundane. It's not an exact science, but I typically strive for a mix of one eye-catching structure for every four to five mundane ones.

Balance and lines

Balance as applied to artwork is the distribution of the visual weight of objects, colors, texture, and space. If the design was a scale, these elements should be balanced to make a design feel stable, **7**. With symmetrical balance, the subjects are essentially a mirror image on both sides of an axis. In the case of asymmetrical balance, the visual weight is similar but not a mirror image. Asymmetrical balance is generally preferable in that it creates more visual interest. The challenge with modeling a railroad is that our man-made elements often lock us into a more "boring," for lack of a better term, symmetrical arrangement, so we need to find creative ways of working around that.

Lines of various types create distinct moods and feelings. A challenge is that the subjects we model tend to be built on engineering order. In other words, 90-degree angles, perpendicular orientations, and parallel lines are the order of the day, **8**. As we discussed in earlier chapters, railroads are linear: rights-of-way tend to be straight, as do streets, fence lines, and utility lines. The scenes we are modeling need to be placed on benchwork that tends to be (or needs to be) more of a straight shelf format.

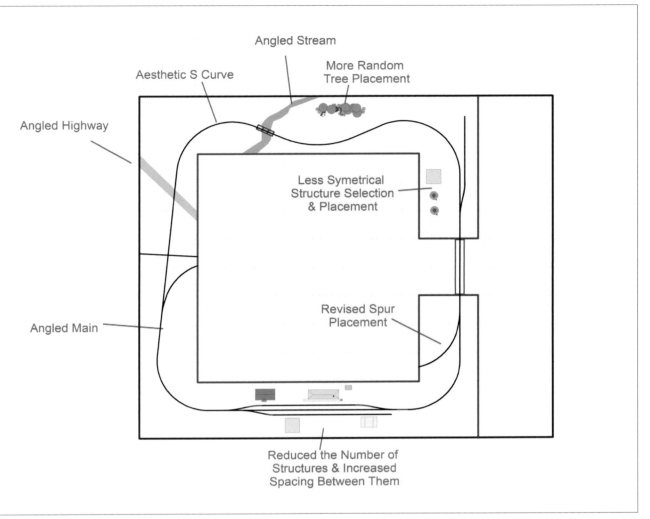

Angled Stream

Aesthetic S Curve

More Random
Tree Placement

Angled Highway

Less Symetrical
Structure Selection
& Placement

Revised Spur
Placement

Angled Main

Reduced the Number of
Structures & Increased
Spacing Between Them

The original plan for a 12 x 14-foot room (left) is sound and would be very straightforward to build—a factor to never dismiss, especially for a beginning model railroader. However, it suffers visually: The track and scenery placement are too symmetrical and the structure arrangement in the town at the bottom too dense. On the revised version (right), we've added angles and gentle S-curves on the main line. Tree placement is less orderly, and structure density is thinned and less uniform. The highway and stream have been angled.

Finally, we have a general tendency as a species to subconsciously create order. When you combine all of these factors, we tend to get a design that looks very "90-degreeish." We can combat this by angling linear elements with respect to the fascia and backdrop wherever possible, **9**.

So far all of our discussions related to curves has centered on the unavoidable need to turn a corner or direction. However, curves can serve an artistic purpose as well. We may be faced with a situation where we have a relatively long, linear run down the benchwork and through a large scene. If it makes sense from a geographic standpoint (an area of the country where you'd

expect some curves), the scene can be enhanced by adding broad-radius, gently sweeping curves or S-curves ("aesthetic curves"), **10**, **11**. Make sure you follow the track guidelines from Chapter 4 when doing so.

Crop or compress?

We're often faced with designing an appealing scene that we want to include, but without quite enough benchwork surface area to do it justice. The natural tendency is to simply squeeze all the elements more closely together so that the scene fits, **12**. However, in doing so we've essentially eliminated the necessary negative space to create plausibility.

Although it takes some discipline, a better approach is to make the hard decision to crop away some of the elements from the scene and maintain the distance between those that remain. In other words, crop, don't compress, **13**.

The simple layout plan in **14** shows how to develop these ideas. The plan revision adds angled track and other elements for interest, and thinned out dense areas. Keep these concepts in mind as you work on your own plans.

1

CHAPTER NINE

Case study: Frederick, Md., 1952

Making four strategic decisions led to an effective design

This 1972 photo highlights street running, as a Penn Central local eases its way northbound up East Street in Frederick, Md. Barely visible in the distance is the Carroll Creek trestle curving to the left. This is the essence of Frederick, and the feeling that Fred wanted to capture on a layout.
Paul Dolkos

In putting this book together, it was important to me to use designs that have actually been built by my clients as opposed to being just pie-in-the-sky intellectual exercises. Many of these are very experienced modelers just looking for an outside detached, guided opinion. These modelers bring a unique perspective in that many have been in the hobby for decades, made their share of mistakes, and are very clear in knowing how long and how difficult various aspects of a design actually take to build.

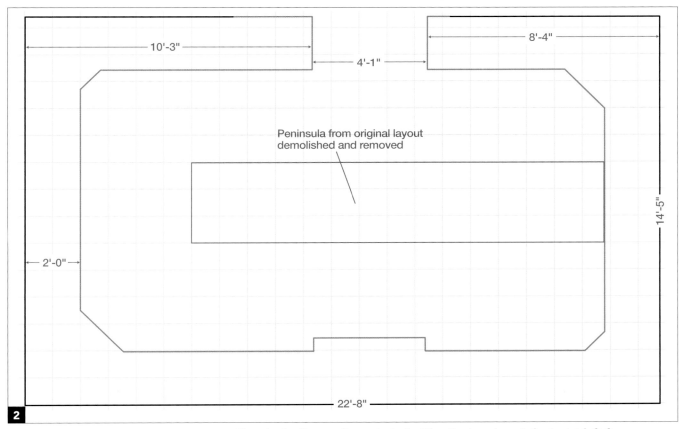

2

Here is the "canvas" we started with—the benchwork footprint left from an earlier layout. The first strategic decision was to scale back the scope by demolishing and removing the old center peninsula. This opened up the room, simplified the scope, and reduced the time it would take to make substantial progress on the layout.

Enter longtime friend and client Fred Scheer. Fred had a dedicated layout room that was already filled with a model railroad. As time wore on it was clear that after a solid 10-year run, the layout had served its purpose and had hit the end of its lifespan. He made the decision to build a new HO scale layout in the same space using most of the existing benchwork to save time. More importantly, he wanted to bring to the process lessons learned, increased self-awareness, and more focused interests. For the new project he went in with the realization that being retired didn't equate to having as much free time as he anticipated, so he wanted to scale back the scope of what he'd bitten off with the last venture. Let's follow the design process following Fred's viewpoint.

Frederick, Md., in the 1950s had caught his attention, **1**. It was a compelling subject, something that resonated with him, something that created enough of an emotional pull that having a miniature version of it would be meaningful. With experience he realized that switching and

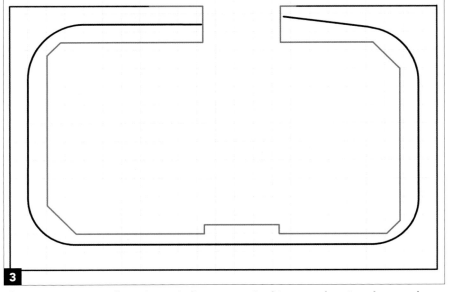

3

The next step is to place the main line route—in this case, there's only one place to put it! We've angled the line at upper right for visual interest and to contrast with the treatment on the left. The nature of a design such as this, where all of the curves are 90 degrees and in the corners, makes the radius less crucial—we used 30" (more than necessary mechanically, but we had the room).

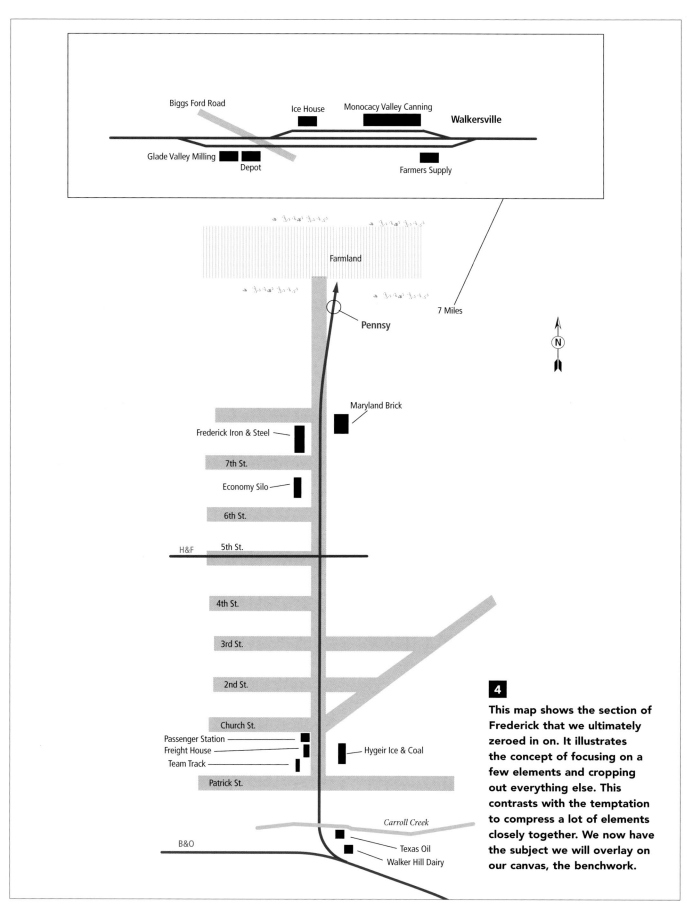

Biggs Ford Road

Ice House

Monocacy Valley Canning

Walkersville

Glade Valley Milling

Depot

Farmers Supply

Farmland

7 Miles

Pennsy

N

Maryland Brick

Frederick Iron & Steel

7th St.

Economy Silo

6th St.

H&F 5th St.

4th St.

3rd St.

2nd St.

Church St.

Passenger Station

Freight House

Team Track

Patrick St.

Hygeir Ice & Coal

Carroll Creek

B&O

Texas Oil

Walker Hill Dairy

4

This map shows the section of Frederick that we ultimately zeroed in on. It illustrates the concept of focusing on a few elements and cropping out everything else. This contrasts with the temptation to compress a lot of elements closely together. We now have the subject we will overlay on our canvas, the benchwork.

5

Along with street running, another key scene is the Carroll Creek trestle. Here a northbound local crosses the span in January of 1972. Several boxcars on the B&O are visible through trees to the right. *Paul Dolkos*

branchline operations were what he found most interesting, so he wanted a platform that would play to that. Boiling it all down to a central, focused objective for the layout, he wanted a sense of being transported visually to Frederick as well as having a sense of being an active participant in that world via realistic switching operations. That was the goal of the layout.

Frederick is unique. It has a big-city vibe within the geographic confines of a small town. As you approach it on the highway, one second you're in cornfields, and the next it's as if you're in the densest of neighborhoods in Baltimore. Then, just as suddenly, you're back in the cornfields again. Within those tight boundaries there was a lot going on in terms of railroading in the '50s. You had the Baltimore & Ohio, the Pennsylvania Railroad, and a fascinating electrified

line, the Hagerstown & Frederick, which crossed the PRR at a street intersection and had an interchange track with the Pennsy.

During that time, Frederick proper was packed with a diverse group of small, very "modelable" industries, interchanges, and details—one key modelgenic scene after another. It would be tempting to try to incorporate them all.

Therein lies the trap, the ambush that lures us in. By attempting to feature more elements than our available space will realistically allow us to pull off visually, we win the battle and lose the war. Left unchecked, the end result of an all-you-can-eat smorgasbord like this can all too often be that toy train set look as opposed to something that captures the unique sense of place that is Frederick. It takes an enormous amount of self-

discipline, but the war is won by identifying the one key attribute that signifies "the place" more than any other—a small scene—and doing that exceedingly well. Yes, many captivating features will be left out, but the gains outweigh the losses in terms of visual balance. Architects and designers often comment that the best designs spring from situations with tightly defined boundaries and constraints. It forces you toward a focused, clean, refined end result where there is a sense of balance and every element serves a purpose.

The point of all of this is that the ultimate success of the Frederick design is attributed to the four strategic decisions Fred made before a line was drawn—and less with curve radius, turnout size, and secondary track design. Let's walk through those four decisions. Note that although Fred

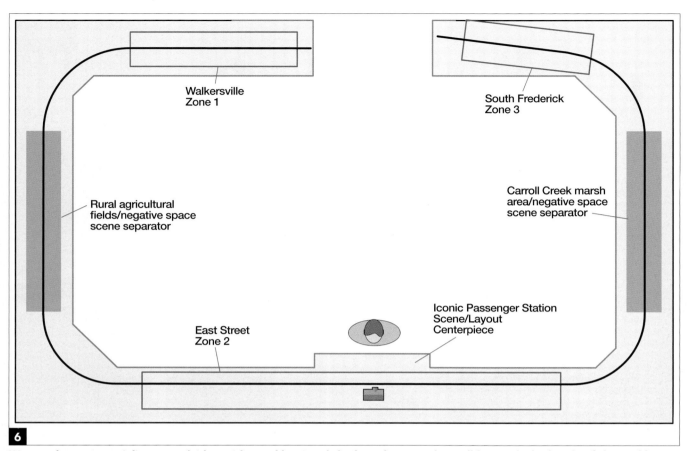

Walkersville
Zone 1

South Frederick
Zone 3

Rural agricultural
fields/negative space
scene separator

Carroll Creek marsh
area/negative space
scene separator

Iconic Passenger Station
Scene/Layout
Centerpiece

East Street
Zone 2

6

We now have our mainline route laid out (the necklace) and the key elements that will be used (the beads of the necklace). At this point it's a matter of overlaying the elements on the route. The exact spacing is a judgment call based on personal preferences, but setting "hard limits" on the size of the negative space will keep us out of trouble. Note that the key scene, the Pennsy passenger station, is located at the central point of the room so that it's the first thing you see as you walk in the room. Since the center of the room is so open, we have space for a bump-out to develop the scene around the station with row houses.

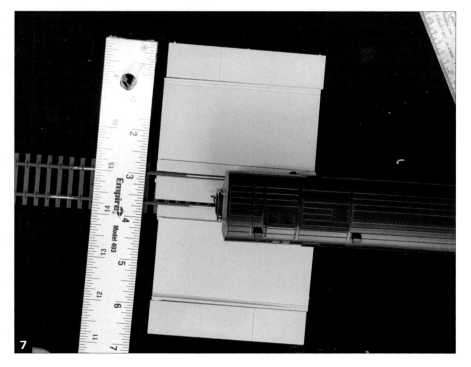

7

It's common to have a crucial aspect of a design that is difficult do work out on paper. In these situations it's helpful to resort to a full-scale, three-dimensional mock up. Such was the case in this plan with the width of East Street. To determine the exact space needed, we used Walthers street track inserts to determine the offset from the fascia to the track center line.

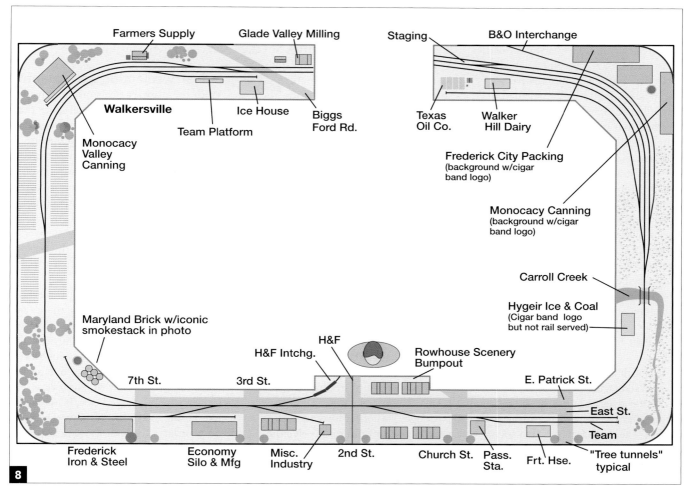

8

The final step was to develop the secondary track and details. We needed a runaround at each end of the line. Actual street widths were used in Frederick to avoid an overly compressed appearance. There is a runaround in the street on the prototype, but we omitted it on the layout because it wasn't operationally necessary and doing so greatly simplified construction. Note the angle to Biggs Ford Road in Walkersville. Also note that we've included industries that aren't rail served.

is a "prototype modeler," this project would be more accurately described as proto-freelance: It has most of the key features of the area, located for the most part in their actual locations, but, if necessary, liberties were taken to make the design work.

After considerable thought, and looking at various scenarios, the most critical of strategic decisions was made: eliminating the center peninsula of the earlier benchwork, **2**. This led to a successful design, and the basic route pretty much drew itself, **3**. Decision two was to model one place—Frederick (although that decision came with a twist, as we'll see in a bit).

Strategic decision number three was to focus the scope tightly and only model a small part of a small

town—specifically just a ¾-mile stretch of East Street between Patrick and 7th Streets. If ever there were a vignette that personifies Frederick, this stretch is it. Iconic and photogenic, this corridor features street running, historic row houses, a variety of industries, a passenger station, and a freight house. This degree of focus meant making the difficult decision to leave some very compelling elements on the cutting room floor: the B&O (other than the interchange), most of the H&F (ouch!), other than a dummy crossing and the interchange, and the other portions of the Pennsy in town. It's OK to cry!

Although East Street is the focal point, we also need some additional supporting elements. Specifically:

staging, an interchange with the B&O, and a few more industries to add time and interest to an operating session. While not particularly noteworthy visually, a several-block area just south of Patrick Street will serve this purpose and be another key zone on the layout. We'll call it "South Frederick." We could now sketch the section of line that we want to model, **4**.

One town but with a twist

As Fred and I worked back and forth on the design, my original focus was keeping the boundaries tightly lassoed around Frederick. Fred pointed out that 7 short miles to the north was the small town of Walkersville. It wouldn't be a stretch to call it a suburb. What makes Walkersville unique is that not only is the rail element there geographically small, it's tightly clustered with model-worthy industries and structures. After some back and forth (i.e. arguing about creative differences), Fred's logic prevailed as he explained that Walkersville was so small that we could easily work it in and still have enough room for negative space to provide a buffer between it and Frederick. Ultimately the decision to include it changed the operational aspect of the design, as now it wasn't a Frederick switching layout but rather a branch line with an emphasis on Frederick. The forth strategic decision was to include Walkersville.

At this point we've established the five elements to be featured on the layout:

1. East Street (the layout's focal point)

2. South Frederick

3. Walkersville

Wait—where are nos. 4 and 5? Remember the importance of negative space/scenery separators? Two such elements are vital to making this plan work, and are *as* strategically important as are the three elements listed. Frederick is an island floating in a vast sea of bucolic agricultural scenes. That geography is a regional identifier, a stamp that tells us where we are. We'll use it as the first of two negative spaces to create a sense of distance between Frederick and Walkersville.

The second scenery-only zone/ negative space buffer will be the Carroll Creek swamplands a few hundred yards south of Patrick Street, **5**. This swampy, mosquito-infested marsh area around the sometime-creek, sometime-raging river separates the East Street street-running scene to the north from the more mundane South Frederick industrial zone to the south, which serves as staging and an interchange with the B&O.

So, rounding out our list, the fourth and fifth key elements to be featured on the layout are:

4. Carroll Creek scene separator between East Street and South Frederick

5. Agricultural scene separator between Frederick and Walkersville

We can now overlay this "necklace" string of elements atop the basic track route, **6**. The exact spacing is a judgment call, but setting "hard limits" on the size of the negative space will keep us out of trouble. The key scene, the money shot of the Pennsy passenger station, is located at the central point of the room—it's the first thing you see as you walk in the room. Since the center of the room is so open, we have space for a bumpout to develop the scene around the station with row houses.

Now's the time to figure out any potential logistical challenges. Since street running is a key, Fred needed to know the exact width of East Street, with track and sidewalks, **7**, to allow for enough room for structures and open space between the street and fascia. Mocking it up full-size allowed precision in the final plan.

Industry selection and quantity

With the primary decisions largely settled, the next step is developing the individual scenes and adding secondary track. For those who want to operate, even on occasion, some key decisions impact the design. First, how long do you want an operating session to last? Will you be operating by yourself or with others? How often will you be having sessions? For Fred the answers were: Solo operator most of the time, weekly operations, sessions that run 30 minutes to an hour.

Since we aren't looking at three-hour sessions with multiple crews, there's no reason to design in switching capacity that will never be used. This gives you the luxury of having fewer industries and spacing those industries out, and takes the pressure off to have every industry be rail served. Yes, it may seem like heresy to say, but not every business on your layout—even those next to the main—need to have a spur. The industries chosen are representative, and we have more than enough to spin out an hour-long operating session plus a cushion. The completed plan is shown in **8**.

A "good design"

In the end we have a design that transports its owner to a noteworthy time and place, **9**, **10**, is buildable in a reasonable timeframe without numerous construction challenges to overcome, takes into account available hobby time, is comfortable to interact with, and satisfies operational objectives. It's visually balanced, doesn't look like a toy, and incorporates some artistic theory (diagonals, negative space, symmetry).

Note that I haven't spent an inordinate amount of time discussing tactical matters such as siding length, turnout size, dimensional data, etc. Although these factors certainly matter, ultimately it is the strategic decisions that are made—not the tactical—that ultimately determines whether a design is successful in the end.

Proto-freelancing

Strictly defined, a truly "prototype" model represents everything to their exact dimensions. The reality of our available space makes that impossible. How far you stray from the real thing is a matter of degree. I will argue though that if you stay too close to the prototype and don't allow yourself some artistic leeway, the design will suffer. And, if you don't loosen the reins it could suffer a lot. A happy middle ground is the "proto-freelance" approach which uses large doses of actual elements from a specific place but gives you the luxury of changing their dimensions, the space between them, sometimes their relative location, and the flexibility of picking and choosing which ones to keep and which ones to eliminate. This approach to composition leans more toward art and aesthetics. Handled well, proto-freelancing will allow you to capture your goal of being transported to that magical place and do so within the very limited boundaries of your available space. Such is the case with Fred's Frederick, Md., layout that we're discussing.

A northbound Pennsylvania Railroad excursion train stops at the Frederick passenger station as it runs northbound up East Street on May 5, 1940. *Norman Perrin; Ernest Colwell collection*

Even though this image is from 1972, not much in this scene has changed since 1954 other than the vehicles and building signs. Note the tight clearance between the train and automobiles. *Paul Dolkos*

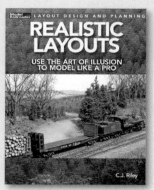
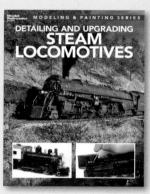
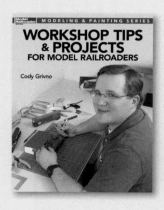